PRAISE FOR *HOTEL* BY JOANNA WALSH:

> Evocative ... Walsh's strange, probing book is all the more affecting for eschewing easy resolution.
>
> *Publishers Weekly*

> Walsh's writing has intellectual rigour and bags of formal bravery ... *Hotel* is a boldly intellectual work that repays careful reading. Its semiotic wordplay, circling prose and experimental form may prove a refined taste, but in its deft delineation of a complex modern phenomenon—and, perhaps, a modern malaise—it's a great success.
>
> Melissa Harrison, *Financial Times*

> Walsh has been praised to the skies by Chris Kraus and Jeff Vandermeer, and it isn't hard to see why. Her writing sways between the tense and the absurd, as if it's hovering between this world and another.
>
> Jonathan Sturgeon, *Flavorwire*

PRAISE FOR *DRONE* BY ADAM ROTHSTEIN:

> Adam Rothstein's primer on drones covers (such themes as) the representation of drones in science fiction and popular culture. The technological aspects are covered in detail, and there is interesting discussion of the way in which our understanding of technology is grounded in historical narratives. As Rothstein writes, the attempt to draw a boundary between one technology and another often ignores the fact that new technologies are not quite as new as we think.
>
> Christopher Coker, *Times Literary Supplement*

OBJECTLESSONS

A book series about the hidden lives of ordinary things.

Series Editors:

Ian Bogost and Christopher Schaberg

Advisory Board:

In association with

LOYOLA UNIVERSITY NEW ORLEANS

Georgia Tech | Center for Media Studies

BOOKS IN THE SERIES

hood

ALISON KINNEY

Bloomsbury Academic
An imprint of Bloomsbury Publishing Inc

B L O O M S B U R Y
NEW YORK · LONDON · OXFORD · NEW DELHI · SYDNEY

Bloomsbury Academic
An imprint of Bloomsbury Publishing Inc

1385 Broadway
New York
NY 10018
USA

50 Bedford Square
London
WC1B 3DP
UK

www.bloomsbury.com

**BLOOMSBURY and the Diana logo are trademarks of
Bloomsbury Publishing Plc**

First published 2016
Reprinted 2016

Library of Congress Cataloging-in-Publication Data
Names: Kinney, Alison, author.
Title: Hood / Alison Kinney.
Description: New York : Bloomsbury Academic, 2016. | Series: Object lessons |
Includes index.
Identifiers: LCCN 2015023231 | ISBN 9781501307409 (paperback)
Subjects: LCSH: Hoods (Headgear) | Hoods (Headgear)–Social aspects | BISAC:
SOCIAL SCIENCE / Anthropology / Cultural. | LITERARY CRITICISM / Semiotics
& Theory. | PHILOSOPHY / Aesthetics. | SOCIAL SCIENCE / Media Studies.
Classification: LCC GT2110 .K54 2016 | DDC 391.4/3–dc23 LC record available at
http://lccn.loc.gov/2015023231

ISBN: PB: 978-1-5013-0740-9
        ePub: 978-1-5013-0741-6
        ePDF: 978-1-5013-0742-3

Series: Object Lessons

Typeset by Deanta Global Publishing Services, Chennai, India
Printed and bound in Great Britain

On March 28, 2012, US Representative Bobby L. Rush spoke on the floor of the House. Removing his jacket and pulling up the hood of his gray sweatshirt, he said, "Racial profiling has to stop, Mr. Speaker. Just because someone wears a hoodie, does not make them a hoodlum. . . . Just because someone is a young Black male and wears a hoodie does not make them a hoodlum. . . . I applaud the young people across this nation who are making a statement about hoodies and the real hoodlums, particularly those who tread on our laws wearing official or quasi-official cloaks."

Representative Gregg Harper said, "Members need to remove their hoods or leave the floor." The sergeant-at-arms escorted Representative Rush from the chamber.[1]

CONTENTS

1 "THAT VERY, VERY SIMPLE THING ABOUT THE HOOD"

I've long believed that the content of fashion does not materialize spontaneously but, in ways both mysterious and uncanny, emerges from the fabric of the times. That fabric has recently been darkly threaded by war and uncertainty.

—ANNA WINTOUR,
Editor-In-Chief of American Vogue[1]

We all wear hoods: judges, athletes, rappers, torturers, politicians, and toddlers. We don hoods to attend school, commute to the construction site or office, go to war or protests, take a hike, walk the dog, ride the Maid of the Mist, or visit our grannies in the woods. We dress babies in animal-eared hooded onesies to enhance their resemblances to other species (and, if we're Anne Geddes, to conquer the world); we zip kids into hooded snowsuits to induce them, infallibly, to pee. Coaches, firefighters, fishers, boxers, beekeepers, and Mark Zuckerberg wear hoods professionally. Skaters, cosplayers, fetishists, presidents, and the entire Knowles-Carter family wear them to play.

It's very simple: everybody with style, everybody venturing out into the rain, everybody not completely resistant to one of the world's most practical, ubiquitous garments of the past couple millennia wears hoods.

The hoods in this book come in wool, polyester, leather, cotton, pasteboard, hide, palm leaves, and plastic. Their designs range from garments we'd all agree were hoods, to objects that stretch the definition, objects we wouldn't call hoods in other contexts. Anne Boleyn's round headdress was a French hood; the Queen of Hearts's pointed headdress was an English hood. Professors in formal academic dress sling gabardine and silk hoods around their necks. At Abu Ghraib, plastic sandbags and women's panties served as hoods. Languages, cultures, practices, several continents, and thousands of years of style mean that, for the purposes of this book, if people are wearing them and can agree that they're hoods, they're hoods. (Sorry, but you'll have to wait for the sequel to get car hoods, stove hoods, and Mount Hood.)

We all wear hoods. In the second century, there lived a man named Docilianus, who loved his hood until he suffered a changing-room mishap at the spas in Roman Bath. He lodged a complaint, inscribed in a lead tablet, for management and for all posterity: "I curse him who has stolen my hooded cloak, whether man or woman, whether slave or free, that the goddess Sulis may afflict him with maximum death, and not allow him sleep or children now and in the future, until he has brought my hooded cloak to the temple of her divinity."[2]

Romano-British mosaics and medieval European pictures of the chilly seasons span a thousand years of people wearing hoods to hunt birds or tend their hogs. Throughout the Middle Ages, farmers, physicians, nobles, scholars, clerks, apprentices, pilgrims, and jesters wore cozy hoods for work, play, warmth, and fashion; "kings also wore gloves on cold days and hats or hoods in rainy weather, but we are rarely treated to pictures of them doing so." Even their falcons wore tiny leather hoods with knots and bells, after Crusaders adopted the practices of Arab falconers. Hoods were such commonplace articles of dress that John Mandeville's fourteenth-century ethnography of the Tartars in Cathay marvels, "Hoods use they none"![3]

European Christian monks adopted the hooded habit from their fifth-century Coptic predecessors in Egypt. Not only monks, but also a variety of other clerics wore cowls made of serge (woolen twill), though the medieval Franciscans fretted about the difficulty of finding colorfast, cheap black dyes for their hoods.[4] Hoods served them for religious business, for protection from the rain or sun, and, at least in *The Canterbury Tales*, for carrying knives and pins to give to pretty ladies. Although black-hooded monks cast a gloomy shadow over medieval death scenes, their presence still implied the bliss of eternal life—or, the bliss of wealth and authority: if you were so lucky as to be the Duc de Berry or de Bourgogne, you'd have a gazillion gorgeous little alabaster pleurants, statues of mourners with hoods cast over their faces, carved to decorate your tomb and celebrate your afterlife. For all this, the comfortable, everyday hood was no more narrowly a symbol of mourning than a hooded raincoat is now.

Who didn't wear a hood? Death. The Grim Reaper. Charon. Father Time.

For, once upon a time in European art history, Death went naked, or whatever the word is, when you're a skeleton with no flesh to cover up, or a transi, an image of a rotting cadaver, letting it all hang out. Hoods used he none! In paintings and sculptures, Death sometimes accessorized with a jaunty crown, a headwrap, a ladies' black headdress, or a clutch of worms wriggling through his eye sockets. Or a thatch of hair, like a toupee, complete with sideburns. Though Death gave us previews of coming attractions, drawing a shroud coyly up over his skull, he had yet to unleash his signature look, the black hood.[5]

Long before Desmond Davis's movie *Clash of the Titans* (1981) depicted Charon as a black-hooded skeleton, the ancient Greeks (who presumably knew best) had seen Charon only as a ferryman holding out his hand for the fare, sometimes wearing a cone-shaped *pilos* hat. For both Virgil and Dante, Charon was an old man with fiery eyes, an image persisting as late as Auguste Feyen-Perrin's *The Boat of Charon* (1863)—although Michelangelo, who moved in mysterious ways, painted Charon as a mustached, muscular Yoda. Two other mythical figures of Death also went hoodless: winged Thanatos appears in ancient Greek art and drama, sometimes as a baby, sometimes a man in a hat or a black robe; the Ankou, the Death-worker of Breton legend, is just a skeleton or a shaggy old man in a hat or shroud (one popular internet photo of a hooded ankou carved in stone dates only to a playful 1995 church restoration).[6] Even the Grim Reaper and Father Time once went hoodless, as did the skeletons of the medieval *danses macabres*. In these murals and engravings depicting processional dances of the quick and the dead, it's not the dead, but the living dancers who wear hoods—also cloaks, hats, shoes, and other weather-appropriate gear—presumably because it's the living who mind the cold. As Death tells the Abbess, in John Lydgate's 1426 "Dance of the Dead":

> And you, my lady, gentle dame abbess,
> With your furred mantles, large and wide,
> Your veil, your wimple of exceedingly great richness,
> And soft beds—you must now leave aside
> For to this dance I shall be your guide.

But maybe Death got cold too, dancing skimpily over the course of the Little Ice Age (1300–1870). In the sixteenth century, he donned some suspiciously hoodlike headgear for Hans Holbein the Younger's *danse macabre* prints, published in 1538 and reissued in hundreds of both authorized and pirated editions. Pieter Bruegel the Elder's painting *Triumph of Death* (1562) captured a moment of symbolic invention and transition, with its black-hooded skeletons, bareheaded Grim Reaper, and, awesomely, a blue jester-hooded skeleton crashing a party like it's 1599. And in a castle in northeast England, even a Jacobean poltergeist who complained "I'm cauld!" was banished by the gift of a warm hood: "Here's a cloak, here's a hood, the Cauld Lad o' Hylton will do no more good."[7]

After Holbein and Bruegel, Hooded Death finally went viral: in Francisco de Goya's spooky *Que viene el Coco* (1797–9), Gustave Doré's *Death Depicted as the Grim Reaper on Top of the Moon* (1845), Dickens's Ghost of Christmas Yet To Come, the French crime fiction villain Fantômas, Disney's Wicked Queen and Maleficent, the Nazgûl, Emperor Palpatine, Skeletor, *South Park*'s Kenny, J.K. Rowling's Death Eaters, Benedict Cumberbatch's Khan—and the Unabomber's WANTED poster. Hooded bereavement spans the permutations of Victorian widows' weeds, Buddhist white sackcloth hoods, Mexico's Santa Muerte, and the Guglmänner, Bavarian separatists who are still mourning the 1886 death of Ludwig II. Charmingly, a study of Swedish healthcare professionals found that "84% of men and 65% of women image [*sic*] death as an old man, usually dressed in dark clothing . . . described most often as a dark cloak or mantle with a hood. The hood is thought to conceal a thin, bony face, which, among 15% of the study group, was said to be that of a skull." Nearly one quarter of respondents referenced Ingmar Bergman's film *The Seventh Seal;* the study doesn't cite *Bill and Ted's Bogus Journey.*[8] (And in the medieval painting of Death playing chess in Täby, said to inspire Bergman, Death isn't wearing a hood.)

But Hooded Death isn't just fun and games of chess. In 1987, a television ad from the Australian National Advisory Committee on AIDS depicted the Grim Reaper at a bowling alley, knocking down people like pins. The Grim Reaper was meant to represent HIV—or, perhaps, to demonize gay men and drug users.[9]

The history of the hood is a *danse macabre*, where the hooded living and dead join hands. We all wear hoods, but our hoods evoke everything from recess and the wind chill factor to executioners and cross burning. They provoke poetry, legislation, and playful or fatal speculations on what exactly hooding means. More often than not, this ambiguity protects the powerful at the expense of the powerless, regardless of who's wearing the hood. Hoods warm the heads of killers, victims, or both at once, confusing motives and the innocent lack of any motive at all, to disastrous and deadly ends, even for nations at war.

We sanctify the executioner with impersonality. We say: He is the hand of the state, and must be protected. He is retaliating, for us decent people, against a man who has left society, a man who has repudiated citizenship by committing the act of murder. Bull, fucking, shit. The executioner is not a figure of vengeance, and his hood is not disguising his identity, because everyone knows who's behind it. The hood is his sanctification, and what it sanctifies is denial.

—**DOUGLAS DENNIS,**
late editor of the Louisiana State Penitentiary inmates'
magazine, The Angolite

Nobody plays the role of Grim Reaper quite like Florida in the twenty-first century. In the 1970s, after a brief national moratorium on capital punishment, many of the states that resumed the death penalty developed elaborate penal secrecy procedures. Florida outdid them all: the state commissioned a "medieval" hood to completely conceal its executioners' identities. Ivan Solotaroff has recorded how, at dawn, a corrections staffer drives to an agreed-upon location to pick up the executioner, already wearing his hood, and escorts him through the prison to the executioner's cubby:

> "It is a strange sight indeed, that man sitting there in his hood," admits the Florida DOC's unusually jocular spokesman, Eugene Morris, whom I speak to several times in an attempt to interview the executioner. "Particularly in this day and age. Not to mention at six in the morning."
>
> "Does he look like something out of the past, in his hood?"
>
> "Yes. I would say so. Very much."[10]

Florida pays its executioners in cash, keeping their names off the accounting rolls, and the death teams may not publicly acknowledge their participation in executions: "Well, we, we were sworn to secrecy. When I first got on the team, I wouldn't even tell my wife what I was doing. The deal was, keep it among ourselves. Whatever we say or do down here has got to stay down here, you know."[11] Even Florida doctors have worn "purple moon suits," with face shields, to hide their identities from the American Medical Association, which bans medical attendance on executions: "We are a profession dedicated to healing," says the AMA. "Participation in an execution is an image of a physician with a dark hood."[12] In 2014, Florida Representative Michelle Rehwinkel-Vasilinda sponsored legislation requiring the disclosure of executioners' identities, but it died in the Criminal Justice Subcommittee.

Although Florida's rituals are extreme by comparison with those of such states as Alabama, where executioners' identities are matters of public record, many states hood their death teams, either literally or figuratively. In South Carolina, executioners "would go into the death house . . . dressed in ponchos, covering their heads, prior to everybody else's getting there to protect their identity"; in Oklahoma, they wear "ghost-like hoods and robes." In 1990, a Washington state court ruled that prison authorities need not disclose the name or qualifications of its new hangman, who refused to do the job if his identity were revealed. Said the judge, "The undisputed evidence is that the state could not proceed with an execution if disclosure were made."[13] Although many executioners don't wear hoods, hooding remains an apt metaphor for many other mechanisms of penal secrecy: technologies that obscure which bullet or switch delivers death, the screening of witnesses, death chamber curtains, recording bans, nondisclosure of executioners' professional competence, and drug and equipment suppliers.[14] All these procedures hood the violence, horror, and guilt of executions, even from the people conducting them, thus allowing them to continue.

Critics often invoke the so-called Dark Ages to explain the tradition behind Florida's "medieval mask and hood." They write, "The hooded executioner anonymously dispatching enemies of the crown may be the stuff of costume dramas, but in Florida the secrecy is reality." For centuries of tradition, they say, executioners have ritually worn black hoods, "to insulate them from the weight of the responsibility of taking a human life," "to prevent their recognition," "to protect their identities, which would offer them a token shield against harm."[15] The evasive theatrics of US capital punishment have struck reformers as "medieval" at least since Founding Father and death penalty opponent Benjamin Rush wrote in 1788, "My essay upon the punishment of murder by death has been attacked in our newspapers by the Revd Mr Annan. . . . His arguments are flimsy, and such as would apply better to the fifteenth than the eighteenth century."[16]

But European execution art tells a different story, a surprising story with surprising consequences for contemporary debates on capital punishment. Like the Grim Reaper, the executioner once went hoodless. In paintings and sculptures of decapitations, burnings, and hangings, executioners have worn kerchiefs, helmets, and all kinds of hats (a top hat, in Théodore Géricault's *Public Hanging in London*, c. 1820), or, in the glorious humanist tradition, nothing at all (Raphael, *The Massacre of the Innocents*, c. 1509)—but until quite recently, no hoods, no masks, no anonymizing headgear. Their faces are fully visible, and in many pictures, the executioner is distinguishable from the spectators only by the ax or noose he holds. Some documented executioners have worn distinctive costumes: in sixteenth-century Nuremberg, executioner and diarist Frantz Schmidt tarted up in a "ruffled collar, a nice jerkin and doublet, and . . . bright colored hose."[17] Mastro Titta, the Papal States' executioner from 1796 to 1865, wore a red cloak and a matching red puffy hat to work, but took off the cloak before mounting the scaffold.[18] Again, no hoods. What, then, of the stigma and anonymity? Says Schmidt's biographer, "This whole idea of a mask . . . it's a joke to think that somehow you were going to remain anonymous—that people in a town weren't going to know who you were." Paradoxically, even the stigma suggests that communities were fully aware of their executioners' identities. In the early modern Dutch Republic, Flanders, and Germany, people often stoned executioners in the street—or solicited them for medical advice, since they had intimate knowledge of how bodies were put together. By the eighteenth century, almost all the Dutch hangmen's families were related to each other;[19] endogamy would have been neither necessary nor practical, if their communities hadn't known who they were. And in Paris, everybody knew that the Sanson family held the office of executioner for nearly two centuries.

The exceptions to executioner recognition prove the rule. Peeter Huybrechts' print of the execution of England's Charles I shows the executioner and his assistant wearing white, owlish masks—the kind you'd be sure to wear, too, if you were committing a highly visible and controversial public regicide. In paintings of martyrdoms, especially medieval crucifixions, executioners do sometimes wear distinctive white coifs (baby-bonnet-like hoods), everyday colored hoods, turbans, and pointy hats. These hoods and hats, though, have been identified by Ruth Mellinkoff as belonging to the Christian iconographic tradition of "Jews' hats." Christians depicted Jewish figures as wearing Jews' hats in order to demarcate and denigrate them. Widespread recognition of the symbol eventually inspired some communities to force their Jewish members to wear actual Jews' hats and hoods. Thus, the medieval artistic "tradition" of hooding martyrs' executioners represents not real penal practice, but the anti-Semitic attempt to make executioners look like stereotypically Jewish Christ-killers. If this weren't obvious enough, later painters would add hooked noses and dark skin colors under the hoods.[20]

This use of the hood should give us pause. It's a representative strategy that recurs throughout the hood's history: authorities, and media-makers, associate the garment with a vulnerable community, then brand that garment as a vehicle for death. Every time Hooded Death makes an appearance, we need to ask whom the depiction benefits, and how. (One contemporary example is the sinister Red Riding Hood murderer of Daphne du Maurier's "Don't Look Now," made into a 1973 film by Nicolas Roeg. The story personifies Hooded Death as a person with disabilities.)

Amidst the jumble of documentation, fantasy, and bigotry, who benefited from creating the symbol of the hooded executioner? Whose lives were at stake? The "historic" hooding of today's executioners is a political sleight of hand, with real, mortal consequences.

Many scholars have chronicled how, starting in the seventeenth century around the world, philosophers, humanitarians, and revolutionaries campaigned to reform or abolish capital punishment. Cesare Beccaria's *An Essay on Crimes and Punishments* (1764) inspired abolition in Tuscany and Thomas Jefferson's work on the Virginia penal code. Reformers argued against cruel and excessive punishment; they advocated privacy, dignity, human rights, professionalization, medicalization, and, above all, the removal of executions from public view, if not their outright abolition. Unfortunately, reformers and authorities collaborated in the invention of such "humane" alternatives to capital punishment as penitentiaries, hard labor, and solitary confinement.[21] Nineteenth-century elite reformers often cared less about the rights of condemned people than about sparing their own delicate sensibilities, or repressing what Bowdoin Professor Thomas Upham called the "great riot, noise, confusion, drunkenness, and every species of crime" of public execution audiences. Anti-populists fretted that the crowd's brutality would lead to copycat crimes, bloodlust, and commercial disruptions. As a result, reform perpetuated what in 1841 the *Democratic Review* called "a private judicial assassination, which shrinks from the open view of the public, and perpetuates its revolting function only within the guarded precincts of the prison walls in the presence of a small number of officials or privileged spectators." Executions moved from the public scaffold to the prison, and from local jurisdictions to states', under the auspices of centralized, professionalized bureaucracy. Throughout the next century, the tightening of procedural, technological, and even interior decorating constraints cut off public access and oversight. The reformers had unwittingly helped create "the wrong remedy"; as Sing Sing warden Thomas Mott Osborne said, "they abolished publicity instead of abolishing executions."[22]

Enter George Cruikshank, caricaturist and illustrator of the works of Charles Dickens (whom he later accused of ripping off his original plot for *Oliver Twist*). Cruikshank's 1840 illustration of the 1554 execution of Lady Jane Grey portrayed a bizarrely fiendish, batlike executioner in a black mask. Cruikshank also depicted the 1606 execution of Guy Fawkes, with the axeman in a black mask under a black capotain hat, and the hangman in a low-drawn, black cavalier hat with a black cape. Cruikshank helped usher in a nineteenth-century fad for painting hooded executioners, retroactively outfitted in fantasy costumes, that diverged from any historical reality; another example is Jean-Paul Laurens's mural of the 1383 execution of the Maillotin rebels, at Paris's Hôtel de Ville.[23] These sinister, hooded executioner images enabled reformers, then and now, to draw self-congratulatory delineations between savage, old-timey executions, and supposedly humane, dignified, superior modern capital punishment—as the *Cincinnati Enquirer* did in 1897, when it crowed that the introduction of the electric chair made hanging "a relic of barbarism in Ohio." This identification of the Middle Ages with barbarism is what Umberto Eco calls "shaggy medievalism," and it's not just medieval scholars who should get mad about it. As Robert Mills writes, "Foucault may well declare that what he terms the modern 'carceral city', with its imaginary 'geopolitics', takes us 'far away from the country of tortures, dotted with wheels, gibbets, gallows, pillories.' But tell *that* to the people being tortured now, in the police cells, prisons, detention centres and execution chambers of—yes—the modern West."[24]

If you can stomach an online search for images of the "medieval executioner," you'll see shaggy medievalism at work (and I don't mean in the bondage gear, which is a realm of play). One of your top hits, cribbed from the 1859 volume *Costumes anciens et moderns*,[25] depicts a man wearing a black robe and full-face black hood with eyeholes. But this illustration is not of an executioner; the original volume correctly identifies him as a comforter, a member of one of many Catholic lay brotherhoods originating in fourteenth-century Italian cities. Comforters visited, prayed with, and escorted the condemned to their executions. They brandished paintings of martyrs before prisoners' eyes to inspire them, to induce docility, and to conceal the sight of the scaffold. The comfort they offered was ethically dubious: in promising heavenly rewards for submission to earthly authority, the comforters smoothed the workings of penal violence. Yet their invocation of martyrdom was unintentionally subversive, suggesting that the condemned prisoners might also be innocent martyrs. In the anonymity of their black hoods, the comforters managed all at once to abet, allay, and question judicial violence.[26] This ethical ambiguity is missing from the stereotype of the savage executioner, but relevant to death teams today, with their emphasis on dignity and decorum.

These quibbles about the comforters' hoods, anti-Semitic hoods, and the neo-medieval Florida hoods aren't just matters of veracity; they're bound up in death penalty rhetoric and politics. The spectacle of the sinister hooded executioner, embodying a brutal, distant past, diverts our attention from the all-too-modern violence of the contemporary execution. It obscures past and present complicity with and resistance to capital punishment. It concentrates all accountability in the single, ghoulish figure of the hooded executioner, while making us feel better about the supposedly just, impersonal, simple, and humane systems we perpetuate now.

That's why we moderns put black hoods on executioners.

If Gary wanted to die with dignity, then he had to respect that very, very simple thing about the hood. It was there for practicality to allow the thing to run very dignified, and no movement. Gary listened in silence.
—Father Meersman persuades Gary Gilmore to wear the black hood for his 1977 execution by firing squad, in Norman Mailer's
The Executioner's Song[27]

Although there's only scanty evidence for the hooding of executioners prior to the late nineteenth century, there's a long tradition of forcibly hooding prisoners. In 1829, the Quaker-style Eastern Penitentiary of Pennsylvania, lauded by Alexis de Tocqueville, required inmates to wear hoods at all times when they were outside their cells, for social control. Eighteenth-century London travel guide writers witnessed executioners yanking nightcaps over the faces of the condemned, prior to hanging.[28] Hoods render prisoners submissive, making it difficult to breathe, speak, or struggle, and impossible to look executioners or witnesses in the eye.

Florida also masks prisoners in the electric chair. Made of leather, the mask's surface is blistered by boiling saliva. One Florida death team leader who role-played the part of prisoner for execution rehearsals said, "It was peculiar, you know, because when they put the mask on me, you know, you can't really tell what the person is doing. You feel helpless." His teammate added, "You feel totally helpless, you can't move, you can't see, you can't speak. It's total darkness. All you can hear are sounds around you. It's definitely weird. It's kinda like puttin' you in another world. . . . You get a little queasy, I guess from being helpless. You can't fight it."[29] In 1772, French murderer François Billiard behaved with such propriety on the trip to the scaffold that he was allowed a hat drawn low over his face to shield him from the crowd's gaze; everybody, including Billiard, regarded the hat as a reward—an even more insidious form of social control.[30]

Besides ensuring prisoner compliance, hoods and masks dehumanize and objectify prisoners in the eyes of witnesses and executioners. Florida's leather prisoner's mask suggested to one executioner the appearance of "a hooded hawk—not a person but a constrained creature, poised, in this instance, for death." Louisiana's executioner from 1983 to 1991 said of killing masked prisoners, "There's nothin' to it. It's no different to me executing somebody and goin' to the refrigerator and getting a beer out of it. . . . They all look the same. It's just a procedure, and they happen to be part of it."[31]

After the US-Dakota War of 1862, a US military commission tried 392 Dakota men and boys in seven weeks and sentenced 303 to death, although President Lincoln reduced the number to 39. In Mankato, Minnesota, the army arrayed the prisoners in rows on a custom-built scaffold, with identical white muslin hoods muffling their faces. The victims, who'd had no lawyers and were prohibited from speaking in their defense during the trials (which were in English, anyway), sang through their hoods. They were hanged all at once, before 4,000 witnesses. It was the largest mass execution in US history. Afterward, the *Sioux War Panorama*, a backlit, hand-cranked moving picture with live narration and music, took images of the execution on a Midwestern tour, including a stop at the St. Paul Opera House.[32]

Hooding prisoners for execution is one of the procedures that create the reassurance of "higher civilization," as a New York doctor attending the first judicial electrocution marveled in 1890: "A party of ladies could sit in a room where an execution of this kind was going on and not see anything repulsive whatever." Or, as the Florida Department of Corrections now annually certifies to the governor, "The procedure has been reviewed and is compatible with evolving standards of decency that mark the progress of a maturing society, the concepts of the dignity of man, and advances in science, research, pharmacology, and technology. . . . The foremost objective of the lethal injection process is a humane and dignified death." Or, as California Governor Ronald Reagan put it in 1973, "Being a former farmer and horse raiser, I know what it's like to try to eliminate an injured horse by shooting him. Now you call the veterinarian and the vet gives it a shot and the horse goes to sleep—that's it."[33]

In 1848, the *American Whig Review* advocated chloroforming the condemned, because their convulsions disturbed witnesses' "nervous peace, which is the support of refinement"; such a disturbing execution was "against good manners, and unbecoming in a civilized Christian people."[34] Such concern for witness sensibility suggested that the witnesses, even the executioner himself, were the most vulnerable people at an execution, while the prisoner was a kind of Grim Reaper, even at the moment of his own death. Former Virginia executioner-turned-abolitionist Jerry Givens once said he found electrocution "more humane" than injection—for the executioner, who thereby felt less "attached."[35] When authorities try to avert "botched" executions such as those in 2014 in Ohio, Oklahoma, and Arizona, it's hard to tell who they're concerned for (note the pervasiveness, and implications, of calling an execution that fails to kill "botched"): during the 1988 execution in which Raymond Landry's arm broke loose and spewed fluids around the chamber, the curtain before the viewing room snapped shut, lest the witnesses be traumatized.

As Sister Helen Prejean wrote, the worst possible injury to execution participants and witnesses is the harm to good conscience. The hooding, pacifying, and sequestering of prisoners conceal not only their pain and suffering, but also the reminder of complicity:

> With witnesses behind the square of Plexiglas like that, it was like a framed scene, death in the movies, death in celluloid, death under glass. There he was, saying his last words. There he was, walking to the chair. There he was, being strapped in. Three clangs of the switch. No smell of burning flesh (the Plexiglas shields witnesses from the smell). No sight of his face (the mask conceals his face, his eyes). And with his jaw strapped shut like that, he could not cry out.
>
> Who killed this man?
> Nobody.[36]

What would happen if the Plexiglas and the hoods were removed? Who, besides the condemned, might cry out?

After Cincinnati's first private execution in 1852, the Reverend George Washington Quinby called the crowds who'd gathered outside "a ragged, drunken, profane, cut-throat appearing crew, of all nations and colors—men, women and children peering through the crevices in the wall—smoking, chewing, drinking and cracking jokes, or each other's heads." This view of the execution mob, which still pervades death penalty rhetoric, was largely invented by reformers. Before then, authorities depended on public spectators to legitimize, witness, and even assist with executions. (Likewise, the stampede for lottery tickets to Timothy McVeigh's execution, and the costumed, pot-banging, effigy-bearing crowds at Ted Bundy's, simultaneously embarrassed authorities and validated the sentences.) What reform really sought to eliminate was the chance of audiences getting too close, seeing through the hoods, and veering off-script.

Before the reforms, public executions sometimes afforded opportunities for crowds, and the condemned, to readjudicate sentences and denounce injustice. In 1761, Parisians rioted to prevent the hanging of a servant who had committed petty theft, begged forgiveness, and returned the stolen cloth. After the crowds had halted her execution, they looted her accuser's shop, then obtained the prisoner's pardon. Audiences from Edinburgh to Prague also assaulted executioners, rescued prisoners from scaffolds and, in France, bought them new suits; they once stole the entire scaffold and gallows in Montreal.[37] Even the most orthodox, institutional witnesses sometimes choose to identify with the condemned. In 1674 in Massachusetts, at Benjamin Goad's hanging for fornication with a female horse, Samuel

Danforth spent half his scaffold sermon denouncing Goad before turning on the crowd:

> If we ransack our own hearts . . . we shall finde such sins with us. . . . The holiest man hath as vile and filthy a Nature, as the Sodomites. . . . Let no man insult over him, nor yet flatter himself in his sins, but let us all learn to fear and tremble before the Lord.[38]

Danforth's intent was to damn everybody, not to excuse Goad; still, he was a Puritan preacher willing to drop all pretensions of superiority to a horse-fucker. By comparison, how does Associate Justice Antonin Scalia live with himself, after claiming that lethal injection was an "enviable" death for Henry Lee McCollum, an innocent man who spent 30 years on death row before his 2014 exoneration?

In seventeenth-century London, Margret Clark was sentenced to death for arson. But just after the executioner had pulled the hood over her face, she yanked it back up herself, to address the crowd. "Gentlemen, I have one thing more to say," she declared, then denounced her accomplice, who'd been acquitted. "I testifie [sic.] before you all, now I am going to Eternity; that he is the very Man [responsible for the fire]." Her speech was later published as a popular broadside that connected her personal story to the larger question of miscarried justice; it happened, because she'd been able to doff the hood and engage with the public.[39]

Nowhere was the importance of audience access, for good or bad, more apparent than in the great exception to the US sequester of capital punishment: the Southern states' continuing, well into the twentieth century, to publicly execute Black prisoners. From 1866 to 1920, 76 percent of judicially executed Southerners were Black, twice their proportion of the population. As in the case of the massacred Dakota men, the authorities had no scruples that witnessing the executions might hurt the audience's sensibility, or even any coherent notions of crowd deterrence or incitement: all were irrelevant to the whole-scale criminalization of Black people and the consolidation of white power. What authorities didn't reckon on was Black communities' transformation of legal murder into opportunities for martyrdom. With hymns, prayers, and the accused's last speech announcing salvation (one, as rendered by the *Birmingham Age Herald* in 1894: "I'se happy ter know that I'se ter die like Jesus Christ—ter save sinners. I'se a 'zample and when I'se gone the folks will say, 'He's gone ter rest; he give his life as a 'zample'"), prisoners and spectators mounted a pious, devastating protest of racial injustice. In 1891, the *New Orleans Picayune* opined that the ideal execution of a Black person precluded his "stating that he would 'go straight to Heaven and know everlasting glory.' . . . There was none of the 'Glory Hallelujah' sensational accompaniment."[40] While some historians suggest that the South finally implemented private executions because the public ones too closely resembled lynchings, Michael A. Trotti argues that the public ones, with their Black witnesses' sanctification and resistance, didn't look *enough* like lynchings to satisfy whites. Indoors, with a private audience, authorities could stage real Jim Crow executions: witnessed only by white men, bereft of redemption, and intended to strike a more mysterious "terror in the heart of the superstitious African," as the *Richmond Times-Dispatch* put it in 1908.

To dismiss all these different crowds as rowdy trouble-makers ("of all nations and colors") oversimplifies popular expressions of empathy, faith, and protest; perpetuates ugly stereotypes; and persists in the state control of witnesses and protesters. Dwight Conquergood described how he and other vigil-keepers had to gather in a fenced corridor, submit to searches, ride Bureau of Prisons buses escorted by guards with rifles, and take a Pledge of Nonviolence: "We will not swear or use insulting language. We will not run in public or otherwise make threatening motions. We will honor the directions of the designated coordinators. In the event of serious disagreement, we will remove ourselves from the Vigil Action."[41] When the Angola warden warned Sister Helen Prejean against creating a circus atmosphere, what kind of stunts did he suppose she might try? And how could her tricks, or those of protesters, be any worse than the violence enacted in the chamber?

If the very, very simple thing about the hood—and about all the figurative hoods of penal secrecy—is the practicality, for allowing things to run very dignified, there's a very, very complicated reality it's trying to conceal. Like the execution of Allen Lee "Tiny" Davis in 1999: a surprise gush of blood from under his black hood belied the facade of cleanliness and dignity, making witnesses and staff gasp in horror. Disturbing post-mortem photos of Davis, with the hood half-yanked off his face, hit the internet, sparked outrage, and made the American Civil Liberties Union request an execution moratorium from Governor Jeb Bush, "until officials can ensure that they can be conducted *humanely*" (my emphasis).[42] Although hoods and other concealment protocols don't always work as intended, they're designed to prevent just this scenario. Otherwise, executions run the risk of reactions like that of NYPD inspector William H. Bell, when he witnessed an 1851 hanging: "It was the most sickening sight that I ever beheld and God grant that I may never have an occasion to witness another execution, and that the death penalty may be abolished and imprisonment for life be substituted."[43]

Then they hood-winked my sons to hang them. . . . They came to hood-wink me also; but I told them, they need not, for I could look them in the faces, and was not afraid to die.

—WILLIAM EDMUNDSON,
founder of Quakerism in Ireland, on his and his sons' nearly being executed in 1690[44]

A prisoner need not be blameless, for a government to be guilty of killing him and trying to hide it. Former President Saddam Hussein's trial was rife with accusations of human rights violations and judicial irregularities, and his execution shredded the final impression of dignity in the proceedings. While his executioners and witnesses wore black masks, Hussein declined to be hooded.[45] The video images of his unhooded, unrepentant, praying face, and of that same face gruesomely contorted, troubled the legitimacy not only of the execution, but also of democracy itself. They unmasked not Hussein's violence—the summary execution by hanging of 148 men and boys—but that of the new government, and of the US, which, upon the entrance of its troops into Baghdad in 2003, had hooded Hussein's statue with a US flag, knotting a noose around the statue's neck.[46]

As Mills argued of medieval execution art, "Images of hanging do not always perform the cultural work of those who hang." Any act of state murder runs the risk of looking like exactly what it is. Some states are more upfront about this: the Vigo County, Indiana, death certificate lists McVeigh's manner of death as "Homicide." What would happen if every execution (not only the ISIS beheadings) went viral and made martyrs of the black-hooded prisoners? What if Hussein's death inspired us to think of "the inescapable barbarity of capital punishment and of the intelligible and conventional reasons why it should always be opposed"?[47]

Principled objection to the death penalty under any circumstances gains momentum, when authorities kill the innocent and the unjustly sentenced. As Camus wrote of the execution of the innocent, "When Hugo writes that to him the name of the guillotine is Lesurques, he does not mean that all those who are decapitated are Lesurques, but that one Lesurques is enough for the guillotine to be permanently dishonored." Activists had already realized, 150 years ago, that authorities not only executed the innocent, but also disproportionately executed poor people and people of color. In 1847 Philadelphia, 1,777 women petitioned the legislature, arguing that the poor were put to death, "while the more wealthy universally escape the penalty." During the 1848 trial of Washington Goode, one broadside pleaded for his life as "a colored man . . . one whom society most preeminently injures—doomed . . . by cruel prejudice and wicked statutes, in almost every part of the country—the child of an abused race," while the *Boston Herald* argued that a "white man who had money" would have escaped the death penalty.[48] Their arguments still hold true, as the Death Penalty Information Center's quarter century of research attests. And the bureaucratic hoodings of capital punishment, from witness control and press gags to armed policing of vigils, all first documented in the nineteenth century, continue to suppress dissent and outrage about this truth.

Two hooded figures face each other, and both their hoods serve power. Hooding works, finally, to protect not the executioner, the executed, or the witnesses to the execution, but the institution of legal murder itself. Authorities use hoods to invoke tradition, to displace violence into the uncivilized past, to deflect attention from death rituals invented in our lifetimes, and to muddle the identities of all involved, regardless of who's wearing the hoods. When Florida costumes its executioner in a "medieval hood" that no self-respecting executioner of the Middle Ages would have worn, it employs both the "medieval" and the distracting hood itself to hoodwink the public about the policies and justifications of state violence. The hooded executioner means so much more than anachronistic fantasy: his hood signifies a willful obfuscation of power—of overt and covert violence and guilt—of the disavowal of responsibility. Such imagining of "tradition" reaches far beyond the museums and picture books, pervading contemporary penal practice, politics, life, and death.

2 THE STRUGGLE AGAINST TERRORISM

They look like normal people, don't they? That's the way they are nowadays—they don't wear hoods anymore.
—**GWENDOLYN CHISHOLM,**
resident of Jasper, Texas, on the white supremacists who tortured and murdered James Byrd Jr. in 1998[1]

Morelia, Mexico, 1934. The first mural, painted in an interior courtyard and then walled up for thirty years, is antic with violence. Hooded, robed figures torture and kill their victims by whipping, hanging, and electrocution; a bound woman hangs in a sack. Two men in white pointed hoods drag a corpse. Workers armed with lead pipe and spiked club rush to the rescue of the oppressed.

Sadr City, Iraq, 2004. The second mural brightens a concrete wall along a busy street—and exudes anticipation and dread. One painted figure, draped in a black hood and poncho, stands on a box, electrical wires attached to his widespread hands. Beside him, the sickly greenish, white-hooded Statue of Liberty holds a switch connected to the live wires.

Painted seventy years apart, across the breadth of continents and cultures, the two murals show us war, torture, and hoods. The hoods of executioner and executed. Klansman and lynched man. Interrogator and prisoner. Torturer and tortured. Artists, from court painters to Hollywood directors, itinerant muralists, and even the torturers themselves, have long chronicled the hood's uses in terror, policy, and propaganda. Snug or pointed, white, black, or multicolored, made of muslin, pasteboard, or plastic bags, their familiar shapes recur in frescoes, photos, and animatronic waterboarding installations at Coney Island, tempting us to pin down their ultimate meanings.[2]

But no hood design means any one, single, exclusive thing. Like the mirrored hoods of executioners and prisoners condemned to death, these hoods reveal not just their wearers' personal choices—or their lack of choice—but also contradictory historical expectations, wrapped up in similar designs. Even the word "hood" is a contronym bearing simultaneous, opposite meanings: hoods suggest both secrecy and obfuscation, and, for judges and scholars, recognition and prestige. Hoods clothe both the powerful and the powerless, either to declare or to conceal people's wills, often against the wills of others. To accurately identify the sources of authority, danger, terror, and difference, when so much turns on a flap of fabric, is the problem of the hood itself.

FIGURE 1 *The Struggle against War and Fascism*, 1934–5, by Philip Guston and Reuben Kadish, the Museo Regional Michoacano, Morelia, Mexico (photographer unknown, 1935). Reprinted by permission of the Reuben Kadish Art Foundation.

FIGURE 2 Photograph of a Mural by Salaheddin Sallat, 2004 (REUTERS/Ali Jasim, 2004).

The hood liners are adjustable so, unless you have an unusual size head, one size fits all.

— *www.kkklan.com*[3]

Long before the artist Philip Guston was celebrated for his cartoonish paintings of pink flesh, cigarettes, and Klansmen (*Riding Around*, 1969; *Poor Richard*, 1971), he was Phillip Goldstein, a member of the Los Angeles socialist Bloc of Mural Painters, and a kid on a road trip. In 1934, Guston/Goldstein, fellow Bloc painter Reuben Kadish, and writer Jules Langsner bought a Ford coupe for US$23 and drove to the city of Morelia, Mexico. Morelia, named for the revolutionary priest José Maria Morelos, was a stronghold of the left-wing politician Lázaro Cárdenas.[4] The university's Museo Regional Michoacano (a former summer palace once occupied by the Emperor Maximilian) had offered the artists a wall to embellish. Guston and Kadish's fresco, depicting swastika, hammer and sickle, cross, whips, nails, and electric chair cap, would go by many titles: *The Struggle against War and Fascism; The Workers' Struggle for Liberty,* as *Time* magazine dubbed it; and *The Struggle against Terrorism.*[5]

The Morelia mural swarms with robed men in peaked white hoods, suggesting one particular kind of terrorism for viewers then and now. But in 1934, when the mural was painted, the Ku Klux Klan's white hood had been standardized for only two decades. How the hood came to be an icon of hatred is the story of image-makers: parade planners and playwrights, Hollywood and the mail-order catalog. Before they came along, though, the early Klan of the postwar South really was an "Invisible Empire," emphasis on the invisibility: covert, decentralized, lacking hierarchy or uniforms, including the now-standard white, conical hood. While some Klansmen did wear white, and later Klan mythology would claim they'd dressed up as Confederate ghosts, they usually drew on folk traditions of carnival, circus, minstrelsy, Mardi Gras—or the mid-century "Calico Indians," hooded and masked farmers rebelling against upstate New York land laws. Klansmen wore gigantic animal horns, fake beards, coon-skin caps, or polka-dotted paper hats; they imitated French accents or barnyard animals;

they played guitars to serenade victims. Some Klansmen wore pointed hats suggestive of wizards, dunces, or Pierrots; some wore everyday winter hoods, pillowcases, or flour sacks on their heads. Many early Klansman also wore blackface, simultaneously scapegoating and mocking their victims.[6]

The lack of a formal uniform helped apologists like John H. Christy, a former Georgia Representative, testify to Congress in 1871: "Sometimes mischievous boys who want to have some fun go on a masquerading frolic to scare the negroes, but they do not interrupt them, do not hurt them in any way . . . stories are exaggerated, and it keeps up the impression among the negroes that there is really a Ku-Klux organization." But pantomime costumes didn't make the early Klan any less real, or brutal: one "colored" witness, Jacob Montgomery of Spartanburg, South Carolina, testified that the Klansmen who pistol-whipped, beat, and kicked him wore "white gowns, and some had flax linen, and some had red calico, and some red caps, and white horns stuffed with cotton. And some had flannel around coon-skin caps." Another witness, Henry Lipscomb, testified that the Klan had killed two of his Black neighbors and one white; they'd stripped, choked, and beaten him, and thrown a fireball into his house.[7] The original Klan, anonymous, unaccountable, and hybrid, springing up in a woman's gown, squirrel skin, or Venetian domino mask, violated its victims, then vanished, denying that any terrorism had occurred.

As Reconstruction ended and Southern white men reclaimed political power, they dropped out of the Klan, no longer limited to secret outlets for their violence. In 1872, the old Klan made a valedictory appearance: in public, in the Memphis Mardi Gras parade, revealing a new kind of pageantry that was no less ceremonial than chilling. Local Klan leaders and representatives from all the Southern states rode their own float, wearing black, conical hats with the skull and crossbones and "K.K.K." in white. They staged the mock lynching of a man in blackface; they lassoed Black spectators.[8] The Klan itself was dying, but only because white supremacy was resurging right out in the open, with the sanction and participation of law enforcement and white society at large. Now they had Jim Crow laws. They had a criminal justice system that disproportionately punished Black people and imprisoned them in prison farms, on former plantations. They had lynch mobs, who no longer concealed their identities.

As Gwendolyn Chisholm would comment over a century later, after the 1998 lynching of James Byrd Jr., the lynchers looked like "normal people." The complete absence of any hood, costume, or concealment presented, literally, a new face of white supremacy. Journalist Ida B. Wells-Barnett estimated that in the twenty-five years after the Civil War, lynchers murdered ten thousand Black Americans. Starting in the 1880s, spectacle lynchings attracted crowds of up to 15,000 white participant-witnesses, who booked special excursion trains to reach lynching sites.[9] They snatched victims' clothing, bone fragments, and organs as souvenirs; they photographed themselves, smiling, posing with their kids beside the broken, burned bodies of their victims; they scrapbooked the photos and mailed them as postcards, confident that they'd never be held accountable for their terrorism.[10] They didn't wear hoods, because they didn't need to.

Lynchings were not spontaneous outbursts of "mob" violence, but the predictable result of institutional support and the outright participation of political elites. The lynchers of Leo Frank, in Marietta, Georgia, in 1915 included a former governor, judge, mayor and state legislator, sheriff, county prosecutor, lawyer and banker, business owner, US senator's son, and the founders of the Marietta Country Club.[11] Frank's atypical case—he was white and Jewish—attracted media attention that thousands of Black victims never received, yet it exposed the ways that elites and authorities exonerated themselves by blaming mob violence on so-called "crackers." Meanwhile, Mississippi governor, later US senator James K. Vardaman said in 1907, "If it is necessary every Negro in the state will be lynched; it will be done to maintain white supremacy."[12]

Vardaman didn't wear a white hood. Neither did the first woman US senator, Rebecca Latimer Felton, who said in 1897, "If it takes lynching to protect woman's dearest possession from drunken, ravening human beasts, then I say lynch a thousand a week if it becomes necessary."[13] They were cloaked, instead, in state power and popular support, and what their platforms concealed was the truth: Wells-Barnett's reporting and the National Association for the Advancement of Colored People's (NAACP) research had disproved the "thread bare lie" of the lynch mob as honorable defenders of white women. Besides the fact that the myth of the Black rapist was a white supremacist fantasy, 70 percent of lynchers didn't even bother to invoke it to justify their violence. Lynchers killed for such alleged offenses as "sassing," wanting a drink of water, being "troublesome," "conjuring," and often, as in the murders of Mrs. Jake Cebrose and an eight-year-old child named Parks, no excuse at all. Yet politicians still defended and abetted lynchers. In 1918, Georgia governor Hugh M. Dorsey wrote to the NAACP, "I believe that if the negroes would exert their ultimate influence with the criminal element of their race and stop rapes that it would go a long way towards stopping lynchings." The "criminal element" he was referring to was Mary Turner, who had threatened to press charges against the lynchers of her husband, Hayes Turner, and of nine other men. The lynchers, as reported by the *Savannah Morning News*, "took exceptions [*sic*] to her remarks as well as her attitude." They lynched Mary, who was eight months pregnant. Journalist Walter White, whose ability to pass as white enabled him to interview the murderers themselves, reported that they had hung Mary upside-down, set her on fire, cut out her fetus and stomped it, then shot Mary's body multiple times. The Brooks County coroner's jury ruled that all the victims had died "at the hands of parties unknown" and closed their cases; a lyncher served as jury foreman.[14]

It was in this context of bald-faced violence and injustice that Thomas Dixon recirculated the myth of the Black rapist, pursued by vengeful robed vigilantes, for his 1905 novel and play, *The Clansman*. For the first edition of the book, the president of the Society of Illustrators, Arthur I. Keller, depicted the Reconstruction-era Klansmen in an anachronistic uniform of white, shoulder-length, face-concealing hoods beneath spiked caps. Dixon's theater costumes adapted Keller's book illustrations and added a conical white hat to the mix. Together they reintroduced pantomime, fantasy, and nostalgia to what had become a horribly commonplace spectacle for white crowds of murderers.

Then Hollywood took charge. In 1915, director D. W. Griffith adapted *The Clansman* as *The Birth of a Nation*, one of the very first feature-length films and the first to screen in the White House. Its most famous scene, the ride of the Klan, required 25,000 yards of white muslin to realize the Keller/Dixon costume ideas.[15] Among the variety of Klansman costumes in the film, there appeared a new one: the one-piece, full-face-masking, pointed white hood with eyeholes, which would come to represent the modern Klan. Maybe it was Griffith who brought those pieces of fabric together in their soon-to-be iconic form; after all, his mother had sewn costumes for his Klansman father.[16] Or, given the heterogeneity of Reconstruction Klan costumes, maybe Griffith got the idea from another source altogether: Freemason regalia. Or maybe it wasn't Griffith's idea at all, but that of Paris-trained, Costume Designer Guild's Hall-of-Famer Clare West,[17] who worked on the film: maybe she had studied the image of the execution comforter from *Costumes anciens et moderns*, or witnessed confraternal processions in the streets of Europe, or just made it up.

What we do know is that the blockbuster popularity of *The Birth of a Nation* gave free advertising to a traveling fraternal order organizer, former Methodist minister, and garter salesman, William J. Simmons. Simmons didn't just organize fraternities; he'd joined fifteen of them, including the Knights Templar and the Masons. The 1915 lynching of Leo Frank had inspired Simmons to form a new anti-Semitic, nativist fraternity. One week before *The Birth of a Nation*'s Atlanta premiere, Simmons received his state charter for "The Invisible Empire, Knights of the Ku Klux Klan, Incorporated." He sold hoods and robes (US$6.50) sewn in a local shop, wrote a handbook—the Kloran—and, in 1920, hired publicists Edward Y. Clarke and Elizabeth Tyler to launch a massive campaign that attracted 100,000 new members in sixteen months. Kleagles, or recruiters, arranged minstrel shows and screenings of *The Birth of a Nation* and other pro-Klan films. In 1921, the Klan opened the Gates City Manufacturing Company in Atlanta to mass-produce regalia imitating *The Birth of a Nation*'s designs.[18] The sumptuous, full-color, mail-order Catalog of Official Robes and Banners advertised all the standardized, factory-made hoods for the new hierarchy: Klansman (white cotton denim hood, red tassel); Terror (same hood, along with a red waist cord); Special Terror (white satin hood, three red silk tassels). Also for sale were ceremonial banners: the catalog's banner samples all represent Red Bank, in the "Realm of New Jersey" (New Jersey had 60,000 members at the peak of Klan membership, more than Louisiana, Alabama, or the original Klan's home state of Tennessee).[19]

With Black Americans' lives already so severely constrained, or curtailed, by Jim Crow law and lynch law, the newly hooded Klan aimed much of its violence against new targets: immigrants from eastern and southern Europe, Jews, Catholics, supposed Bolsheviks, and unions. The new Klan courted mainstream Protestant, nativist, white supremacist respectability; senators, Supreme Court justices, and governors joined up. So did white women: shortly after the ratification of the Nineteenth Amendment, the Klan auxiliary organization "Women of the Ku Klux Klan" formed. The Vermont Historical Society owns a celebratory women's hood from that time, made not of denim but of softer, finer muslin; it's mended in several places, as though it had seen hard wear. (In the 1919 film *Heart o' the Hills*, Mary Pickford dons a Klan hood to join the nightriders.)[20]

The new hooded uniforms and the secret rituals harked back, not so much to the Klan's early history, as to other fraternal orders, like the Masons. Anonymity wasn't quite the point: while the hoods could assure their wearers' personal anonymity, their force came from declaring membership in a safe, privileged identity that was anything but secret. The hoods made Klan membership cool; they helped rebrand the Klan as a popular, patriotic, money-making white clubhouse movement. Over the next few decades, the

Klan would morph again, going bankrupt and facing tax evasion charges, then reviving, diminished in numbers but ferociously violent, as an anti-Black terrorist organization during the Civil Rights Movement. But as the Klan waned or regrouped, the hooded uniform remained, sometimes anonymizing acts of covert violence, sometimes adorning a public, unconcealed, violent group identity. Either way, the hood signaled the interrelatedness of white supremacy, civic leadership, theatrics, and more or less overt terrorism.

Yet it wasn't only the Klan who organized club networks in the first decades of the last century. The Anti-Lynching Crusaders, an organization of Black club women, raised thousands of dollars to run national newspaper ads to support the anti-lynching Dyer Bill: "Do you know that the *United States* is the *Only Land on Earth* where human beings are *BURNED AT THE STAKE?*" In July 1917, 10,000 Black citizens, first 300 children, then 5,000 women dressed in crisp, starched white, then men in military uniforms, silently marched down Fifth Avenue in New York, bearing banners: "Mr. President, why not make America safe for democracy?" "Mother, do lynchers go to Heaven?" "Give us a chance to live."[21] Black social networks supported not only the journalism of Wells-Barnett and White, but also the anti-lynching work of poet Jean Toomer and playwright Angelina Weld Grimké.

And with so many lives assailed by the white nativist majority, new alliances formed. The NAACP founders who picketed *The Birth of a Nation* included W. E. B. Du Bois, along with Jewish Americans Joel Spingarn, Lillian Wald, Jacob Schiff, and Rabbi Stephen S. Wise;[22] songwriter Abel Meeropol wrote the Billie Holliday dirge, "Strange Fruit." When in 1931 the Scottsboro Boys, nine teenagers framed for rape, faced a lynch mob, then a legal lynching in the courts, the Communist Party USA mounted their legal defense.

The Morelia muralists Guston and Kadish—Jewish, communists, artists—had witnessed Klan rallies, union busting, and cross burning in a Jewish man's yard; red-baiting police ransacked Kadish's family home in 1928. (Another leftist muralist of the 1930s, Thomas Hart Benton, painted *Parks, the Circus, the Klan, the Press,* depicting the Klan's grip on Indiana politics, for the 1933 World's Fair.) When Guston and Kadish participated in the Los Angeles group art show "Negro America," in solidarity with the Scottsboro Boys, the LAPD's Red Squad raided and confiscated the artworks. After a lawsuit forced the return of the art, Guston found his painting of a Klansman flogging a Black man to be riddled with LAPD bullets to the victim's eyes and genitals.[23] Arriving in Mexico a few months later to paint *The Struggle against War and Fascism,* they depicted white- and black-hooded torturers and executioners who represented Klansmen, and so much more besides. The Morelia mural employed the Klan hood, that most flamboyant and secretive aspect of bigotry, to indict the brazenly bare-faced millions: the lynchers, the de facto lynchers of prisons and courts, the senators who threatened to filibuster the anti-lynching Dyer Bill, the police, juries, and complicit neighbors—an unhooded empire that was only too visible.

At nine a.m. on February 7, 1601, the Inquisition of New Spain, in what today is Mexico, sentenced Rodrigo Franco Tavares, suspected Judaizer, to torture, so that he might "tell and confess entirely the truth." In the rack, during six turns of the crank and six cinches of the garrotes on his limbs, Franco screamed, murmured, and sobbed fourteen variants of, "Oh, My God, My God, My God, I have already told the truth on my death, I swear it." Then, according to the Inquisition's scribe, the executioner "placed a linen hood over his head and began to pour a large jar of water forcing it through the hood into his mouth. Once they poured about a quarter of the jar, they took off the hood and asked him again. He said, 'I have already said it and that is the account that I will give to God.'" The executioner waterboarded him a second time. Franco was still protesting, when they returned him to his cell at 10:30 a.m.[24]

In Morelia, Kadish and Guston's mural has yet another name, and the hoods another meaning: *La Inquisición*.

All Monty Python jokes aside, the Holy Office of the Spanish Inquisition was a 400-year campaign for racial purity. Like Jim Crow law, it was implemented not by mobs, but by the painstaking, exacting legal work of jurists; like "lynch law," which killed dozens of Black women and white Republicans, yet mostly murdered Black men, the Inquisition would try suspected heretics, Moriscos, Protestants, and gender nonconformists over its long history, but initially, heavily targeted suspected Jews. (Much of the violence against Moriscos, in the form of military attacks and mass expulsions, fell under the purview of different, non-Inquisitorial authorities.) Like other institutions that enforce injustice through procedure, the Inquisition conducted a great deal of rigorous lawyerly work to promulgate the idea that Jewish people had "sangre manchada" (stained blood) that resisted purification by baptism. This went for their descendants, too: even generations after their ancestors' conversion to Christianity, the descendants remained "New Christians" or "conversos," who'd supposedly inherited the stained blood, with all its stereotypical associations of treachery, heresy, and danger to the kingdom. After years of pogroms, forced conversions, expulsions, and "purity of blood" statutes barring New Christians from civic, professional, and university life, Spanish New Christian practice ranged from furtive observance of Judaism to devout Catholicism. But Spanish royal and ecclesiastical authorities weren't necessarily concerned with the actual beliefs of the accused. Although the Inquisition's avowed purpose was the extirpation of heresy, every trial included an examination of the accused's lineage, equating heretical subversion with stained blood: an analogue to both racial profiling and the one-drop rule.

Compared to other early modern judicial bodies, the Inquisition was moderate in its infliction of torture and capital punishment. What made it terrifying was that, in its persecution of New Christians, it wielded the exclusive, absolute authority to define and criminalize the accused's identity, beliefs, and intentions. Even for the most Catholic of conversos, disproving "heresy" accusations could be as hard as disproving their descent.[25]

Many New Christians fleeing Iberia moved to Mexico, Peru, Brazil, the Philippines, or India, only to find that the Inquisitions, too, went transcontinental. In 1639, the Lima Inquisition arraigned almost a hundred New Christians, punishing over sixty and burning eleven at the stake; in the 1640s, the New Spain Inquisition would arrest 150. The twentieth-century Mexican viewers had all this in mind when they looked on the hooded torturers in Guston and Kadish's mural and renamed it *La Inquisición*. Maybe some had seen Diego Rivera's 1929 Inquisition mural in Mexico City. In the 1970s, maybe they also thought of filmmaker-artist Alberto Isaac's 1977 cartoon in *El Sol,* upon the Klan's announcement that it would detain immigrants at the Mexico-US border.[26] But the Morelia viewers also had a strictly local context: in 1537, the Inquisition of New Spain had tried a prominent Morelia dignitary, Gonzalo Gómez. The charge: Judaizing, or practicing Judaism, after baptism. The evidence: witnesses accused him of engaging in art criticism—he'd called a mural of the Last Judgment "fanciful and contrived"—and drying chili peppers on the arms of crosses.[27]

"Inquisition" was also Guston and Kadish's shorthand for anti-Semitic practices dating from the Middle Ages to the 1930s. Their traveling companion, Jules Langsner, told *Time* that their mural's left and right halves depicted the "Medieval Inquisition" and "Modern Inquisition." In addition, Ellen G. Landau's work highlights an obscure aspect of the Morelia mural: to the side, a black-and-white cartoon panel commemorates the Jews of Trent. In 1475, the leaders of the city of Trent accused the Jewish community of killing a Christian child to use his blood for Passover, a pervasive anti-Semitic accusation called the "blood libel." One Trent victim died in prison, six were burned at the stake, and the two youngest were baptized, then beheaded. A German printmaker, Albert Kunne, printed and distributed a broadside of the massacre, in which the Jewish victims wear white, brimmed hats coming to points with little knobs (very like the "Jews' hats" from other anti-Semitic artworks), while their torturers also wear white hats, with rounded peaks. Four hundred and fifty years later, in a decade when the Nazi newspaper *Der Stürmer* was reviving blood libel accusations yet again, Guston and Kadish copied Kunne's picture, with all those white hats, alongside the main wall in Morelia.[28] "This medieval inquisition hat ignited something in me," said Guston, who was obsessed with art, such as that of Piero della Francesca, depicting what he called the "kneeling figure with inquisitional hood."

Shaggy medievalism alert! Once again, the terminology should give us pause. The massacre of the Jews of Trent wasn't related to either the medieval inquisitions (papal tribunals concerned with heresy) or the *modern* Spanish Inquisition of 1478 to 1834. While his language encapsulated a long, violent history of Christian anti-Semitism, it also obscured the specificity of perpetrators' agendas and victims' sufferings. More significantly, as with the hooded executioner, such language obscures and distracts attention from the ongoing horror of modern violence. And what did Guston mean by an "inquisitional hood"? The torturers of the Morelia mural's main panel wear pointed, face-concealing hoods in black and white. The Jews of Trent wear white pointed hats; their torturers *also* wear tall white hats. Klansmen wear white pointed hoods. Throw in the Inquisition, and the symbols get even more complicated: inquisitors and their victims all covered their heads, but the designs expressed a world of difference between authority, orthodoxy, and violence on the one hand, and suffering, persecution, and death on the other.

The white, pointed cap of the Inquisition, familiar from Francisco de Goya's art, was worn not by inquisitors, but by the condemned. Inquisitors sentenced victims to flogging, galley slavery, or execution, and more often to the auto-da-fé. This was a public shaming for which victims were dressed in a pointed pasteboard hat/hood (*coroza* or *capirote*—the words are sometimes used interchangeably, though they imply different designs) and a white or yellow tunic (*sambenito*). Inquisitors sometimes sentenced victims to continue wearing the *sambenitos* on Sundays, or to hang them from the rafters of their parish churches; this would proclaim the victims' stained blood, long after their "reconciliation" with the church. The peaked *corozas*, which strongly suggested Jews' hats, had no facial masks, because Inquisition victims didn't enjoy the luxury of shielding their faces from the public.

The people who did wear Klanlike, pointed, face-masking hoods in the medieval and early modern periods were those Christians who didn't worry about running afoul of the Inquisition. Catholic confraternities, such as the execution *conforteria*, wore and still wear such *capirote*-hoods.

"Wearing the hood gives me a certain freedom. I'm on the same level as everyone else, exactly the same. That's what the hood is all about—hiding your identity and going from being an individual, to being a part of a collective," confraternity member Antonio Banderas has said.[29] Penitents, like those in Goya's *Procesión de disciplinantes* (1812–19), also wore *capirotes*, to enjoy being hooded in private-public piety: they could anonymously scourge their bodies, while parading the streets—or, during the fourteenth-century Black Death, while massacring Jewish victims. Like confraternity members, penitents came from the noble and middle classes, and their hoods signaled the opposite of the *sambenito*: both their self-debasement and their acts of anti-Semitic terrorism were voluntary, more or less orthodox, and countenanced by their elite social positions.[30] Their hoods, despite the design similarities, would never have been confused with the Inquisition victims' *sambenitos*.

Even within a limited array of designs, hoods' meanings depend on context. Guston and Kadish's depiction of a hooded priest lurking over a bound corpse suggested a welter of additional meanings in Michoacán, where the 1926–9 Cristero War had recently pitted anticlerical government forces against the popular uprising of peasant and Catholic rebels. It's no accident that the mural would be whitewashed and hidden for thirty years after its commission. And the artists were hardly the first or last people to mix up their hoods. The internet is a trove of pointy-hooded inquisitor art, much of it sourced from anticlerical critics who viewed all hooded religious, particularly the inquisitors, as murderous and cultish (from 1519: the Inquisition friars "use their hoods to cover every sort of egregious and nefarious crime . . . confident that laymen and temporal rulers . . . have no power over them.")[31] Popular images of cone-hooded inquisitorial torturers include the sensational century print, *The Scourging of George Penn During the Spanish Inquisition,* from a Victorian reprint of John Foxe's sixteenth-century anti-Catholic *Book of Martyrs*; Louis Ellie Dupin's Inquisition torture scene, republished in the Enlightenment bestseller *Religious Ceremonies of the World*;[32] and Gustave Doré's *Torture by Water* (1865), depicting the wrong hoods, but rightly indicting waterboarding. The Inquisition's reputation for terror may persist today, not because of concern for anti-Semitism, but because of anticlerical torture porn. (See, too, Edgar Allan Poe's "The Pit and the Pendulum," and Giuseppe Verdi's 1867 opera *Don Carlo,* where the Grand Inquisitor dispenses sinister marital advice.)

There's also superficial irony in the fact that the second wave of the Klan adopted hoods reminiscent of Catholic devotions. However, both the Inquisition and the Klan were terror machines, generating violent fantasies of racial origins and contaminations. The Inquisition largely invented what Irene M. Silverblatt, invoking Hannah Arendt, called "the race-thinking blueprints of modern geopolitics": the hierarchies of ethnic, color, class, national, religious, ideological, and sexual identities that paved the way toward modern colonization, slavery, and genocide. The Klan could hardly have arisen without such race thinking.[33] Also, if many fantasy images of the Inquisition cast the white-hooded figures in the wrong roles, conflating modern Jewish victims with medieval torturers, this only underscores the Inquisition's ideological force, even today. The Inquisition represented its victims as defilers and criminals, and the church, state, and blood purity as the true victims—and we reproduce it in our images, costuming torturers in white pointed hoods. The hoods didn't *belong* to the converso victims—they were forced upon the victims as instruments of punishment and so, properly speaking, belonged to the Inquisition—but that's all the more reason to be careful about the identification. The minstrelsy of victimhood, played by those who wield power, is sometimes literal: Klansmen in blackface, or costumed as Catholics *and* Mexican Jews; the similar hooding of executioners and the executed. Depictions of the hood, worn on the correct heads or not, serve particular interests. Five hundred years ago, the inquisitors succeeded in branding their *sambenito*-wearing victims as threats. In 2014, a Zazzle shop sold Louis Ellie Dupin's topsy-turvy picture of white-hooded torturers as a Christmas tree ornament.[34]

I do not like their coming. Now I think on't,
They should be good men, their affairs as righteous.
But all hoods make not monks.

—Queen Katherine
is, rightly, suspicious of Cardinals Wolsey and Campeius's
religious politics, in Shakespeare's Henry VIII

So what did the hooded inquisitor look like? Exactly like the other clerics of his order, in the same hats or hoods. The first Grand Inquisitor, Tomás de Torquemada, wore the white habit and black-hooded cloak of the Dominican friars for work, leisure, and sentencing suspected Jews to burn at the stake. Cardinal inquisitors, such as Fernando Niño de Guevara, from El Greco's *Portrait of a Cardinal* (c. 1600), wore cardinals' red birettas, squarish little hats. The Franciscans who conducted the New Spain Inquisition wore their customary dark, hooded habits. But if inquisitors wore everyday clerical headgear, their dress also made an ideological point. Their appearance of normalcy signified orthodoxy and judicial power, in contrast to the accused New Christians, who were made to look abnormal and frightening in *sambenitos*.

Inquisitors directed all aspects of the tribunals: arrests, gathering evidence, ordering torture, extracting confessions, and sentencing; they held defendants in secret locations, withholding both the charges and the denouncers' identities. What they did not do was crank the rack, administer the waterboarding, or light the pyre. They relegated torture to the torturers, and "relaxed," or handed over, executions entirely to the secular authorities, who, like other executioners of their day, didn't generally wear hoods; in 1524, the Inquisition in Madrid expressly forbade the city executioner to wear a mask or sheet.[35] Yet the scariest participant in an auto-da-fé wasn't the lackey with the torch, but the presiding cleric-judge authorizing the violence. The victims would have been right to view their black clerical hoods in the light of a death squad.

The black hood, consolidating the roles of judge, priest, torturer, and executioner, still haunts the imagination and practice of the law. European judges once wore the same hooded gowns, as did other members of the medieval academy and church (there's a reason why judges, priests, and professors at graduation look alike); their black gowns bear the symbolic vestiges of that image. Modern executioners and torturers wear, or don't wear, black hoods, in response to shifting relationships between official violence and the public. Fearful suspicion of the black hood today ought to show the slippage between the vilified executioners and torturers, and the sanctioning bodies of state power who supposedly keep their hands clean—like US Supreme Court Associate Justice Hugo Black, who joined but later repudiated the Klan; he united the symbols of black-and-white hood, just like the sinister figures of the Morelia mural.

As recently as the nineteenth century, English judges wore the "black cap," a black wig cover, when passing death sentences. In 1884, the Scottish *Journal of Jurisprudence* crankily debunked the practice as a "great deal of nonsense" that mistook judges' hats for a nonexistent, single-purpose death hood.[36] However, the UK judiciary's website notes that, while the 1969 abolition of capital punishment makes the practice obsolete, "High Court judges still carry the black cap, but only on an occasion where they are wearing full ceremonial dress." In Pamela Branch's 1951 crime novel

The Wooden Overcoat, a defendant worries that the judge might whip out the black cap for his sentencing: "The Judge had it tucked away somewhere handy. Somebody had put it there that morning, ironed out freshly, just in case. Who laundered it? Did they wear a different one every time? Who made them and how much were they and who paid?"[37]

Lest anybody regard the judicial Grim Reaper as an anachronism, judges wearing face-concealing black hoods presided over Peruvian military trials until 1997. The judges claimed that hoods were necessary for protection against reprisals. Six years later, a UN human rights investigation found that Peru's anonymous, hooded judges had imprisoned 4,000 people on trumped-up terrorism charges after closed trials that lasted sometimes only a few minutes, where defense attorneys were denied the opportunity to cross-examine witnesses.[38] Who was it who'd needed the protection? In 2004, Raed Jouhi al-Saadi, the judge presiding over Saddam Hussein's first appearance before the Iraqi Special Tribunal, invoked the criticisms of the Peruvian courts' hooding in his decision to let his face, and the "face of Iraqi justice," be televised.[39] His decision had implications graver even than the considerable danger to him and the other judges: the legitimacy of the state itself was at risk. A state may hood its judges, but in so doing, unmasks conflicts of judicial independence, accountability, and transparency. All the same, the ostentatious, and brave, decision to publicly unhood judges serves its own rhetorical purposes: to represent the form of justice, regardless of how justice is carried out.

Hooded Death's continued employment in governance muddles law, might, complicity, and resistance. This is particularly so when powerful interests wield the right to determine when the black hood signifies justice and prestige, and when it means criminality and danger. Often, the interests determining the hood's meanings are the same ones dealing death.

It was hard to see the photos of the torture in Iraq because I too was tortured. I saw myself naked with my feet fastened together and my hands tied behind my back. I saw my own head covered with a cloth bag. I remembered my feelings— the humiliation, pain.

—**HECTOR MONDRAGON,**
a Colombian economist tortured by an officer
trained at the US-run School of the Americas, responding to
the Abu Ghraib photographs[40]

Executioners, inquisitors, torturers, judges, and Klansmen wear hoods as an expression of power, whether they act inside or outside the confines of legal violence. The anonymity of the hoods benefits them, to exalt, protect, and collectivize their purposes. For victims of the auto-da-fé or death chamber, the opposite happens: they don't necessarily choose to wear those hoods; the hoods aren't "theirs." Forced hooding strips them of individuality and autonomy, hides their suffering, causes pain and panic by suffocation, and simultaneously brands them with aberrant or criminal identities. The pieces of cloth may look identical, may even switch from the torturer's head to his victim's, but significance and survival depend on who's doing the hooding. Sartorial decisions, choices to wear or to force others to wear hoods, can serve as weapons of war.

1902: After winning independence from Spain, which had imposed the Inquisition among other colonial repressions, the First Philippine Republic is occupied by the United States. US troops torture Filipino insurgents with inquisitorial waterboarding techniques. President Theodore Roosevelt comments, "The enlisted men began to use the old Filipino method of mild water torture, the water cure. Nobody was seriously damaged."[41]

1940s: At the German concentration camp Fort Breendonk, in Belgium, the mostly Jewish prisoners "sometimes wore handcuffs and had shackles on their feet attached to an iron ring in the wall. They could not leave their cells without being forced to wear hoods. One of these prisoners, M. Paquet, states that he spent eight months under such a regime; and when, one day, he tried to lift the hood to see his way, he received a violent blow with the butt of a gun which broke three vertebrae in his neck."[42]

1950s: Hélène Gautron testifies about victims of French torture at the Villa Sésini in Algiers, including: "Madame Helié (50 years old), 12 hours forced standing, hood over her head, slapping, menacing by dog; . . . Salima El Haffaf, electricity, water, slapping; Fatima Ben Osmane, electricity, water, slapping; Madame Cardi, Claudine Lacascade, student arrested for distributing banned papers like *Liberté* and the *Voix du Soldat*."[43]

1960s–1980s: The Archdiocese of São Paulo reports that US and British advisers have taught torture techniques to the Brazilian militarized police who capture and execute political prisoners. One technique is the "Viet Nam": the torturers hood their prisoners, and force them to stand barefoot on cans, applying electroshock whenever victims begin to collapse from fatigue. Captives seized from their homes at night are hooded; by day, they're put into opaque wraparound sunglasses, so as not to look too conspicuous in public. The violence workers wear hoods of their own, face paint, or fake beards, and call each other "Pompeu," to suggest the indistinguishable corpses at Pompeii. One violence worker, Jorge, said he was glad to switch from doing "stupid things" (torture) to the neater, impersonal violence of summary executions. He could wear his own hood, or put one on a victim; it didn't really matter.[44]

1970s–1980s: During Argentina's Dirty War, prisoners are kept hooded and shackled in the prison section called the "capucha" (the hood). Human rights lawyer Laura S. says:

It was raining, and I was in a hurry to get the kids off to school. "*Capirotes! Capirotes!*" I urged them, in a sudden panic. They had no idea what I was talking about. But I couldn't bring myself to say, "*Pónganse las capuchas,*" or "Put up your hoods." *Capirote* is totally archaic, rarefied. It means "hood" but no child would know that. For me, *capucha* is a place, and that place meant torture and ultimately death for people I loved very, very much.

"Capirote" is, again, the hood of the confraternities and penitents, often identified as the garment of the Inquisition victims. "Capucha" also refers to the rubber, plastic, or cloth hood or bag, soaked with toxic chemicals, used for suffocating prisoners in Argentina. Argentine advisers teach the technique to Guatemalan and Honduran torturers.[45]

1990s: "People are afraid of the unknown. They are afraid of being tortured, of being held for a long time. Try to see what it is like to sit with a hood over your head for four hours, when you are hungry and tired and afraid, when you are isolated from everything and have no clue what is going on," says Michael Koubi, former chief interrogator for the Israeli General Security Services. Interrogators employ hooding alongside forced standing, beating, and shackling of Palestinian prisoners to painfully tiny "kindergarten" chairs.[46]

(Speaking of chairs, briefly, instead of hoods: when Monty Python's Spanish Inquisition threatens a prisoner with "the comfy chair," they're onto something. The CIA's 1963 Counterintelligence Interrogation manual says, "An overstuffed chair for the use of the interrogatee is sometimes preferable to a straight-backed, wooden chair because if he is made to stand for a lengthy period or is otherwise deprived of physical comfort, the contrast is intensified and increased disorientation results.")[47]

2002: In February, US President George W. Bush declares that "the Taliban detainees are unlawful combatants and, therefore, do not qualify as prisoners of war under Article 4 of Geneva," although Geneva does offer limited protections to detainees. And, um, "al Qaeda detainees also do not qualify."[48] The administration bolsters its arguments with shaggy medievalism—"feudal" combatants are ineligible for Geneva protections—and hopes for a replay of the mass execution of the white-hooded Dakota warriors. Army Judge Advocate General, Major General Thomas Romig, later says, "[Deputy Assistant US Attorney General] John Yoo wanted to use military commissions in the manner they were used in the Indian wars. . . . I looked at him and said, 'You know, that was 100-and-something years ago. You're out of your mind; we're talking about the law.'"[49]

US forces regularly strip, shackle, and hood prisoners with smothering black cloth hoods. Guantánamo interrogators find that hooding will "isolate [prisoners] and increase feelings of futility."[50] In the summer of 2002, a prisoner named Mohamedou Ould Slahi is flown to Guantánamo:

> The belt was so tight I could not breathe. . . . One of the MPs was shouting, "Do not move, Do not talk," while locking my feet to the floor. I didn't know how to say "tight" in English. I was calling, "MP, MP, belt . . ." Nobody came to help me. I almost got smothered. I had a mask over my mouth and my nose, plus the bag covering my head and my face, not to mention the tight belt around my stomach: breathing was impossible. I kept saying, "MP, Sir, I cannot breathe! . . . MP, SIR, please."[51]

In August of 2002, the Department of Justice's Office of Legal Counsel clears the CIA to use "enhanced" interrogation techniques on the prisoner Abu Zubaydah, including slamming into walls ("a rolled hood or towel . . . provides a c-collar effect to help prevent whiplash"), stress positions, sleep deprivation, and waterboarding, which "produces the perception of 'suffocation and incipient panic,' i.e., the perception of drowning." A medical officer writes:

> Longest time with the cloth over his face so far has been 17 seconds. This is sure to increase shortly. NO useful information so far. . . . He did vomit a couple of times during the water board with some beans and rice. It's been 10 hours since he ate so this is surprising and disturbing. We plan to only feed Ensure for a while now. I'm head[ing] back for another water board session.[52]

That month, interrogators waterboard Zubaydah at least eighty-three times. In December, Secretary of Defense Donald Rumsfeld approves the Guantánamo Joint Task Force's general request to employ stress positions, isolation, shaving, stripping, and "the placement of a hood over the detainee's head during transportation and questioning." He scrawls below his signature, "I stand for 8-10 hours a day. Why is standing limited to four hours?"[53]

2003: The Guantánamo procedures transfer to Abu Ghraib prison in Iraq. A prisoner named Abdou Hussain Saad Faleh testifies in January 2004:

Then he brought a box of food and he made me stand on it with no clothing, except a blanket. Then a tall black soldier came and put electrical wires on my fingers and toes and on my penis, and I had a bag over my head. Then he was saying "which switch is on for electricity." And he came with a loudspeaker and he was shouting near my ear and then he brought the camera and he took some pictures of me, which I knew because of the flash of the camera. And he took the hood off and he was describing some poses he wanted me to do, and the [sic] I was tired and I fell down.[54]

It is an image of carnival weirdness: this upright body shrouded from head to foot; those wires; that post that recalls, of course, the crucifixion; and the peaked hood that carries so many vague and ghoulish associations. . . . It stands for all that we know was wrong at Abu Ghraib and all that we cannot—or do not want to—understand about how it came to this.

—PHILIP GOUREVITCH AND ERROL MORRIS,
Standard Operating Procedure[55]

Abdou Hussain Saad Faleh, known worldwide as Hooded Man, was one among many prisoners tortured and hooded with dark plastic sandbags, or women's underwear, at Abu Ghraib. (W. J. T. Mitchell observes that the Bush administration's racial stereotyping of shame "explains why, when there were shortages of all basic necessities at Abu

Ghraib, there was an ample supply of women's panties to be used as hoods.")[56] Yet Faleh's photographic image was among the most iconic. The snapshots of the hooded prisoner, and of the soldier admiring his own photography, evoked for some viewers scenes of other horrors: insouciant lynch mobs smiling for group shots beside their victims; the medieval iconography of Christ as the martyred Man of Sorrows, arms positioned at four and eight o'clock; the police torture of Abner Louima; and, indeed, the Inquisition.[57] Abu Ghraib's military police, echoing the paranoia of the Inquisition toward Jews and the Klan toward Black men, regarded their naked, shackled, hooded prisoners as "terrorists" and felt victimized by them. Specialist Megan Ambuhl summarized their attitude as, "Don't turn your back on anybody, because they're all possible terrorists, even the children."[58]

The "ghoulish" and familiar associations powerfully evoke connections between injustices past and present, but they ought also to warn us. As Nicole Archer writes, "Focusing too narrowly on the visual and patently iconic dimensions of hooding limits responsibility for those acts that the hood has come to represent. It shifts conversations away from the materiality of specific, institutionalized techniques of torture."[59] Such a focus also shifts conversations away from everything else that the Bush administration never meant to reveal. Although the photos inspired worldwide revulsion, anger, and protest, they had the collateral effect of abetting the authorities. As Gourevitch and Morris wrote, "The exposé became the cover-up." The investigations that followed resulted in convictions of the MPs, but not of the interrogators who'd directed them, or the superiors who'd commended them, up the chain of command to the generals: nobody above the rank of sergeant served jail time.[60]

And the famous viral photos attracted public attention, at the expense of the victims of crimes that were never photographed. Although the iconic photos of hooded Faleh document outrages on their own terms—sexual abuse, threat of death, humiliation, corporal punishment—too narrow a focus on them obscures other acts, for which evidence must be found elsewhere: the beating of prisoners with broomsticks, the rape of a man with a chemical light, and forced masturbation. And, the incarceration of children in a combat zone, the dog attack on a fourteen-year-old boy, the rapes of women, including the repeated rape of a fourteen-year-old girl, and the bloodying of prisoners by interrogators—civilian, military intelligence, OGA (or Other Government Agency, generally the CIA).[61] On the same night as the photographing of Hooded Man, CIA interrogator Mark Swanner killed another prisoner, Manadel al-Jamadi. The autopsy report: "A hood made of synthetic material was placed over the head and neck of the detainee. This likely resulted in further compromise of effective respiration. . . . The cause of death is blunt force injuries of the torso complicated by compromised respiration." This hooded man was beaten and murdered. Specialist Sabrina Harman, who took forensic photographs of al-Jamadi's body, was charged with tampering with evidence; Swanner was not charged.[62]

The photos, Hooded Man's among them, were made to assist in a hoodwinking of the public, as insidious as the prosecutor's claim that what happened at Abu Ghraib was "Standard operating procedure—that's all it is," or Rumsfeld's cavalier dismissal of "the 'torture' word."[63] The Abu Ghraib photos weren't able to testify to the fact that 70 to 90 percent of these hooded prisoners, according to the Red Cross, were random roundups of no intelligence value or danger. Or that innocence itself was a moot point, when prisoners continued to be detained even after their charges were dropped.[64] The photos cannot represent all the prisoners at Bagram, Guantánamo, and the CIA black sites, whose detentions and tortures were inevitable consequences of the Bush administration's denial of human rights, which, as Judith Butler writes, "institutes the expectation, registers the expectation, that these prisoners are less than human. . . . In this sense, their status as less than human is not only presupposed by the torture, but reinstituted by the torture." Or as Lieutenant Commander Charles D. Swift of the Judge Advocate General's Corps, US Navy, put it, "All men have rights, including the right to a trial—a regular trial! The abuse of prisoners indicates that we don't think detainees are human."[65]

This is hoodwinking: the authorities punished a few culprits, while continuing to build "a worldwide network of prisons, detention centers and surrogates ranging from private contractors to authoritarian foreign governments. . . . The new torture complex—centered in the executive branch of the government but with tentacles throughout the country."[66] The 2012 Senate study of the CIA's post-9/11 detention and interrogation program made horrifying revelations, but there was so much it couldn't reveal: the thousands of still classified pages; the future of dozens of prisoners still trapped in the oubliette of Guantánamo; and the unaccounted-for prisoners whom the CIA has disappeared by extraordinary rendition to foreign governments, for outsourced torture (by such means as electrocution, stretching, and the five-day starving and chaining of a pregnant woman), whose sufferings fall outside the scope of both the Torture Report and President Barack Obama's 2009 Executive Order Ensuring Lawful Interrogations.[67] Not to mention, the ongoing consequences of the invasion of Iraq, which the Bush administration justified with false intelligence about chemical and biological weapons, elicited by torture.

Major General Antonio M. Taguba wrote in 2008 that

> "the Commander-in-Chief and those under him authorized a systematic regime of torture. . . . After years of disclosures by government investigations, media accounts, and reports from human rights organizations, there is no longer any doubt as to whether the [Bush] administration has committed war crimes. The only question that remains to be answered is whether those who ordered the use of torture will be held to account."

They're still free: Jay S. Bybee, John C. Yoo, Alberto R. Gonzales, John Ashcroft, Condoleezza Rice, Donald Rumsfeld, Dick Cheney, George W. Bush. Naomi Klein wrote in 2005, "This impunity is a mass version of what happens inside the torture chamber, when prisoners are told they can scream all they want because no one can hear them and no one is going to save them."[68]

At Abu Ghraib, the hood tortured, shamed, concealed, and disappeared prisoners; later it helped shield the perpetrators and policymakers on the scene and at the Justice Department. Hooding, and outrage over the hooding, served as a cloak, behind which systems of massive state violence remained intact. Maybe that's why the image of Hooded Man remains so horrifying. Hooded Man's hood made him both visible and invisible, in ways that benefited those systems. First it anonymized and dehumanized Faleh. Later, it universalized him as a faceless symbol, isolating him among the best-known victims and relegating many others to the background.[69] Finally, it distracted the public from atrocities, policies, and conflicts still ongoing, now under a Democratic administration. (Critics scoffed at the absurdity of designer Adam Harvey's 2013 anti-drone hoodie and hijab projects. They might rather have asked what his project suggested about the disregard for the lives of the hundreds of people, including 200 children, killed by US drones in Pakistan and Yemen.)[70]

Even so, the hood assumes a slippery symbolic vibrancy. To use Robert Mills's formulation again, hooding, used to inflict suffering and cover up the evidence, does not always perform the cultural work of those who hood. (It's slippery indeed, because the image can also warp expressions of protest and empathy, such as the pervasive recasting of the torture hood as hijab, or the projection of other faces onto the blank canvas of Faleh's hood, erasing the particular politics and violence of his imprisonment.)[71] Still, the official narratives can't entirely control the meanings of Hooded Man's image; it evades containment and still sparks outrage. Among many voices raised in protest, artists have reasserted Faleh's humanity, and that of so many other victims, by reframing their images and exploring their particularity and universality, visibility and invisibility. Qassim Sabti's Baghdad exhibition "Abu Gulag Freedom Park" included Hanan Al-Abeidi's plaster sculpture of a hooded woman, cut open to show a chained fetus, commemorating the raped prisoners; also, Abdel-Karim Khalil's *A Man from Abu Ghraib,* a series of marble sculptures of naked, hooded, bound prisoners, carved months before the media disclosures. "We knew what went on at Abu Ghraib. The pictures did not surprise me." Faleh's black-hooded figure reappeared in 2004 on the freeways of Tehran, as a billboard-style sign, "Emrooz Iraq" ("Today Iraq"), and on an overpass in Los Angeles, in FreewayBlogger's posters *The War Is Over.* In 2007, Iraq Veterans Against the War staged a performance-protest in which soldiers in fatigues hooded and detained prisoners on the streets of New York.[72]

One artist spoke to these protests, but also to the other image-makers, whose hoods echo or defy each other: Bruegel's Death, Goya's Inquisition victims and flagellants, Cruikshank's executioners, Griffith's Klansmen, Guston and Kadish's mixture of them all—and Abu Ghraib photographer Staff Sergeant Ivan Frederick's man of sorrows. This artist was Salaheddin Sallat, another professional muralist, who painted on a concrete wall in the Baghdad suburb of Sadr City in 2004. He chose a street where, he hoped, "everyone can see it."[73] Neighbors and children watched him work. He painted the Statue of Liberty, hooded like a Klansman, turning on the electric current to torture, or murder, Hooded Man. Like the Morelia mural, Sallat's painting is a *danse macabre*, with a live connection between power and the powerless, Klansman and Lady Liberty, America, Iraq, the invisible authorities, and the unmemorialized dead. Both the torturer and the victim wear hoods, white and black, in an uneven, unjust struggle of disastrous consequence for the lives involved, and for the nations they represent.

And Sallat painted text: "That Freedom for Bosh." Because Abu Ghraib was Bush's vision of freedom. And because Bush, and many others, went free.

Sallat's doubled hoods are reminders of all that the photos cannot reveal: the undocumented war crimes, the impunity of policymakers, even the satisfaction of believing that we have witnessed, understood, and protested all there is to know. We haven't. The hoodwinking continues, in The Struggle against Terrorism. La Inquisición. The Struggle against War and Fascism.

3 LITTLE RED RIDING HOODLUM

Tatterhood sailed off, and steered her ship right under the land where the witches dwelt. . . . When the king's men came down there, they saw never a living soul on board but Tatterhood, and there she was, riding round and round the deck on her goat at full speed, till her elf locks streamed again in the wind.

—**"TATTERHOOD,"**
the Norwegian fairy tale where a gray-hooded, goat-riding princess battles trolls and witches to undo the spell that's turned her sister into a calf

In the late nineteenth century, revisionists rewrote the memory and history of the US Civil War. They erased the centrality of slavery to the conflict, erased racial injustice and violence, and promoted a narrative of patriotic, sympathetic brotherhood between white Northerners and Southerners. This reconciliation, whose terms ennobled and justified the

Confederacy, was effected at the expense of Black Americans. The continuities between enslavement and the systemic injustice of Jim Crow in the post-Reconstruction South got brushed aside. Conveniently, this rhetoric was promulgated just in time to recruit droves of reconciled white Southerners for the latest federal colonial projects: the Spanish-American War, then the Philippine-American War.[1]

Whatever the new Southern recruits were expecting to find in the Philippines, it probably wasn't a secret society of hooded Filipino revolutionaries carrying "KKK" banners: the Kataastaasan Kagalanggalangan Katipunan ng mga Anak ng Bayan (Most Noble and Respected Union of the Sons and Daughters of the Country). The Katipunan dressed in black and green hooded robes for secret lodge initiations, signed pledges in their own blood—and fought a two-year war for independence from Spain, then a three-year insurgency against US imperialism. These were Filipino multicultural hoods, which synthesized the legacy of Spanish Catholicism's hooded friars, penitents, and inquisitors, with trendy international fraternities like the hooded Masons. Their meanings also collided, in many ways, with those of the US soldiers who adopted inquisitorial methods to hood and waterboard the Filipino rebels. Maybe white Southern soldiers were inspired by the secret KKK hoods to go home and join the Klan, or the Masons? Twenty-one Black American soldiers defected to the Filipino resistance, refusing to fight their "colored cousins": Did they debate with their new comrades about the KKK banners?[2] Maybe the designs even influenced the Klan propagandizers Thomas Dixon, D. W. Griffith, and William J. Simmons—so that David Duke, Grand Wizard, would unwittingly dress up as an anti-imperial Filipino freedom fighter?

The hood is an object of such longstanding utility and popularity that any significant hood may wind up being worn for a completely unrelated or completely antithetical purpose. For as long as powerful forces have weaponized hoods, forcing them onto the heads of victims or wearing them to conceal their own violence, other people have relied on hoods' anonymity and everyday ubiquity in order to fight back, escape, and protest. In seventeenth-century Vilcabamba, the chronicler and Augustinian monk Antonio de la Calancha fretted that beautiful Incan women freedom fighters were cross-dressing in monks' hoods, in order to seduce and foil Spanish missionaries: stop a moment to consider the boundless subversion of that notion.[3] Both individuals and movements can find that their own uses of the hood run up hard against prevailing ideas of what hoods are supposed to mean. But even when, and sometimes because, authorities brand the hood as criminal or illegitimate, people keep wearing their hoods for resistance, revolution, and transformation, for self-expression, defiance, and play. And, simply to conduct their own private business in spite of what authorities would have them do, which is not the least form of resistance.

Maybe it's this tendency, as much as the association with the Middle Ages, that explains why hoods figure so prominently in myth, fairy tale, fantasy, and dystopia, with their metamorphic conflicts between good and evil, authority and anti-authoritarianism. The Celts had the hooded fertility figures of the three Genii Cucullati (three spirits, or gods, or eggs, or penises—what's the difference?—wearing hoods); the ancient Greeks had Telesphoros, a hooded wellness god. The fourteenth-century Norse *Bard's Saga* features a gray-cowled giant-troll-human hero. The *Nibelungenlied*'s magic hooded cloak (a *tarnkappe*, whose form varies over centuries of retelling), stolen from Alberich, endows Siegfried with "the strength of twelve" and, ahem, subtlety: he "wooed the splendid woman with great subtlety, since the cloak was of such a kind that without being seen any man could do as he pleased in it." Hooded hobbits, dwarves, men, elves, and Ringwraiths populate Tolkien's Middle-earth. *The Man Who Fell to Earth,* a.k.a. David Bowie, wears hooded (spoiler, but it's not like you didn't *know*) alien getups in his quest for water; so do the Fremen of Frank Herbert's *Dune.* The Wonka Vision Oompa-Loompas dance and terrify you in hooded white protective suspender suits. The comics teem with hooded characters, notably Marvel's villain The Hood, who steals his *tarnkappe* from an Alberich-like demon, and DC's anarchist Robin Hood superhero, the Green Arrow. (Wouldn't we love to talk about how Robin Hood's transformation—from aristocrat, to outlaw, to agent of wealth distribution—complicates what we think we know about lawfulness and dissent? Sadly, although Errol Flynn wore a hood on the balcony, Robin's non-engagement with actual hoods merits only a regretful note.) In some feminist versions of "Little Red Riding Hood," including the Merseyside Fairy Story Collective's and *Buffy the Vampire Slayer*'s, Hood faces harassment and assault, but kicks ass, and sometimes dons her assailant's skin. In Angela Carter's version, Hood and Wolf knock boots, which is another kind of transformation.[4] *E.T.*'s Elliott wears a red hoodie when his gang of desperados escapes the feds, smuggling an alien in his bike basket. And Luke, Leia, and the Jedis wear hoods—as does the Emperor—because we all wear hoods, whether we turn to the Dark or Light side of the Force. (So do the Jawas, though their only allegiance is to junk.) On top of everything else, hoods are about transformation, resistance, and everyday life.

James H. Johnson delightfully narrates such a transformative, ordinary day in the Venetian Republic, when all the patrons of the Thistle Café were wearing the head-to-toe ensemble called the *baùta*: the *baùta* proper (a close-fitting black hood), cape, tricorne hat, and mask. This black, hooded costume had developed from a century-long battle between the Venetian Commissioners of Display and the aristocracy. During the 1707 financial crisis, the Commissioners had attempted to maintain aristocratic distinction, quash sumptuary excess, and ban sartorial individualism by decreeing that noble men wear togas in public. Instead, some nobles adopted the *baùta*: cheap enough for poor nobles to vie in style with the rich, while capacious enough to cloak the newfangled foreign wigs and suits the sneaky rich wore underneath. As more patricians donned anonymous black *baùtas*, and state enforcers found it impossible to tell them apart, the subversive trend mainstreamed into the new noble uniform. The commoners followed suit, until, in 1793, nobody could identify the class of any given *baùta*-wearer. Or the gender.

One Thistle Café patron sat reading the *Gazzetta Urbana Veneta*. The newspaper had printed an editorial by "Signor Lover-of-Beauty," who denounced the covering of women. "You women—you who are the beautiful half of mankind— who bring delight to all men who see you . . . why do you deform yourselves in this way?" The reader, whose name was Laura, grabbed a pen to fire off a reply to the *Gazzetta*; the paper published her letter ten days later:

> Will you refuse to read further if I tell you I am a masker? . . .
> You are reading the words of a woman. Without the aid
> of the mask, do you think I would be able to write? The
> gentlemen around me all think I'm a man. They leave me
> in peace to scratch out these lines without annoying me
> with their elaborate bows and handshakes and the pretty
> little phrases whispered in my ear and all the other artful
> things that men do when they talk to members of my sex.
> The delight of responding to you therefore comes from
> the very thing you so scorn.[5]

Laura's hooded, masked *baùta* freed her to read, write, and trounce a male writer, while occupying a (presumably!) male-dominated public space.

Two centuries later, a woman emerged from the surf at Sydney's Bondi Beach, wearing a black-hooded, head-to-ankle outfit. It was a modest, halal, or Islamic swimsuit, of the kind designed and sold by Muslim women entrepreneurs: California microbiologist Shereen Sabet designed the Splashgear modest hooded scuba suit, and Australian Aheda Zanetti trademarked the Burqini, as modest swimsuits are popularly known. The Burqini is a two-piece swimsuit notable, among the variations of modest dress, for featuring not a veil or scarf, but a quick-drying stretch hood, the "Hijood," which Zanetti first sewed for a netball-playing niece. (It also evokes the French silent film icon of cool, Irma Vep.) Zanetti designed a red-and-yellow Burqini, emblazoned with the words "SURF RESCUE," for Mecca Laalaa, who in 2007 learned to swim, then became Australia's first Muslim woman lifesaver, as well as a spokesperson on immigration, assimilation, and beach culture.[6]

Wasaṭī jurists give the green light to women who want the literal freedom of movement Burqinis provide (to amateur, non-competitive swimmers, for Egyptian athlete Sahar Elrefai offers one caveat about the Burqini: "You can't do professional swimming with [a Burqini] because it's just too heavy").[7] Their approval doesn't sway critics like Mayor Alain Kelyor of the French commune of Emerainville, which in 2009 banned a Muslim woman from wearing modest swimwear at the public pool. "All this has nothing to do with Islam, because the pool policy forbids swimming completely dressed, for hygienic principles, like with shorts," Kelyor said, adding, "this isn't an Islamic swimsuit, this kind of swimsuit doesn't exist in the Koran." Although French notions of pool hygiene require a minimalism that has frightened more than one foreign tourist, the Burqini ban did rather evoke the French national ban on full-face veils, instigated that same year.

A statement from Switzerland's right-wing *Démocrates suisses* clarifies the politics of hygiene: "Burqinis are not hygienic, and they constitute a provocation on the part of migrants who don't want to adapt to local customs." One director of public pools in Zurich replied, "The polemic around the burqini is a false problem." Because Burqinis are made of the same fabric as divers' and competitive swimmers' long suits, which provide superior glide, he added, "The hygiene argument doesn't hold."[8]

But the woman photographed in 2011 at Bondi Beach was British food celebrity Nigella Lawson, who is not Muslim. The tabloids wondered if she was converting to Islam, afraid of skin cancer, hiding fat, or being coerced by her then husband, Charles Saatchi, who in 2013 would be seen throttling her in a restaurant. The nasty conversation that ensued castigated hijab as anti-feminist, opined that middle-aged women were too unattractive to wear more revealing swimsuits, and demanded that Lawson stop wearing her "terrorist" outfit. One surprise result was a surge in modest swimsuit sales to Muslim and non-Muslim women alike; apparently, women believed that they had the right to cover up at the beach for whatever reasons they chose.[9]

In 2013, a German court ruled that Burqinis provided adequate modesty and religious accommodation for Muslim girls at school, imposing a Burqini against the will of a Frankfurt student seeking exemption from co-ed swim classes.[10] With all these conflicting arguments about secularism, Islamophobia, compulsion, feminism, and misogyny, what's apparent is the preoccupation with surveilling and controlling women's bodies, hoods, and religious, personal, and gender expression. People are often uncomfortable with others who, for whatever reasons, negotiate their own relationships with their hoods.

It was just such negotiation over a different kind of hood that inspired the *amauti* project. When Veronica Dewar first attended a meeting of the Indigenous Women of the Americas, fellow attendees identified the association's top priorities as craft commercialization and intellectual property protections. Under Dewar's leadership in 2001, the Canadian Inuit women's organization Pauktuutit worked to protect Inuit designs for the *amauti*. The *amauti* is a custom-fitted woman's parka with a hood capacious enough to carry a toddler. Rhoda Akpaliapik Karetak, a cultural adviser and seamstress, says:

> *Amautiit* are an important part of our lives; they not only protect against the cold, but they are also used for carrying babies, helping to develop bonding and understanding between the mother and her child. . . . Mothers were able to continue with their work while carrying their child. . . .

The *amauti* perhaps also served as a method of birth control. For as long as the child remained in the *amauti* they were breast-fed, reducing the mother's fertility. . . . An *amauti* is a joy to have, and there are all sorts of ways to make your *amauti* nice.[11]

At least a millennium ago, and probably for longer than that, many peoples of the Arctic produced superb all-weather, breathable, hooded gear technology. One twelfth-century grave site (NB: a research site monitored by the Iñupiat community) in northern Alaska uncovered the body of a little girl, already training in fabric arts, whose family lovingly buried her after dressing her in a lightweight bird-skin parka with a decorated hood. By the 1400s in Greenland, the Thule people, progenitors of the Inuit, stood warmly, cozily by, while the Norse in their sodden wools shivered, languished, and eventually abandoned their settlements. When Captain Cook voyaged to the Aleutian Islands in 1778, Arctic gear was still so boss that he bought waterproof gut parkas for all his crew; by 1999, when the parka and anorak had already been appropriated, a designer for Donna Karan very nearly pirated the *amauti*.

Pauktuutit attempted to invoke the Convention on Biological Diversity in Canada to prevent further appropriations. As one activist commented, "I have a deep belief that the amauti project is culturally and financially important to all Inuit from East, West, and North. . . . Ideas are like hardy plants. Deep dormancy, many years of no growth, and then one spring you notice new growth. It is the hope you give and I thank you for it."[12] But their protections project has had to be discontinued. *Amautiit*, which were and are worn by Inuit women in Canada, Alaska, and Greenland, are becoming increasingly popular among non-Inuit parents, so Inuit craftswomen urge customers to buy from Inuit-owned businesses that honor their communities' stake in collective, traditional knowledge.

Pauktuutit sought to protect the hood designs of a millennium of seamstresses. Margret Clark, on the scaffold, doffed her hood to denounce injustice; Laura the Venetian masker and lifesaver Mecca Laalaa wore hoods to claim public space and open dialogues. Hoods can play transformative roles in people's movements, speech, and declarations about what exactly they, and their revolutionary costumes, mean.

Sometimes, while she's at it, the hood-wearer tries to transform the whole world.

Who are those hooded hordes swarming
Over endless plains, stumbling in cracked earth
Ringed by the flat horizon only
What is the city over the mountains
Cracks and reforms and bursts in the violet air
Falling towers
Jerusalem Athens Alexandria
Vienna London
Unreal
      —T. S. ELIOT, *"The Wasteland." Yes, I went there.*[13]

In the 1930s in Rochester, New York, the Knickerbocker Knitting Company renamed itself Champion Knitwear and attached a hood to a sweatshirt. *Ecce* hoodie! Champion sold its hoodies to upstate football teams, tree surgeons, and other outdoor laborers.[14] Over the next few decades, athletes, surfers, *Rocky*, hip-hop and graffiti artists, skaters, college students, and a big dose of advertising transformed the hoodie into mainstream style. Meanwhile, Champion underwent its own transformation, eventually acquired by Hanes Brands, which manufactures or contracts its garments in facilities in the Philippines, China, Vietnam, Haiti, El Salvador, and Honduras. In 2011, the International Textile Garment and Leather Workers' Federation named Champion among sixty companies that failed to pay living wages for workers; their report documented other abuses of workers' rights such as below-minimum wages, retaliation against unions, pregnancy tests on women workers, and child labor violations. Who benefits from these practices? For context, in 2004 the *Hartford Courant* found that the US$37.99 price on a university-branded Champion hoodie comprised $1.37 in fees, $8.32 for the manufacturer, $6.85 for Champion, $21.27 for the University of Connecticut—and $0.18 for the factory workers.[15]

Sometimes, though, hoodies come back to haunt the corporate globalizers who profit from them.

On November 29, 1999, when 45,000 people convened in Seattle to protest the World Trade Organization's (WTO) ministerial meeting, it was no surprise that many wore black hoodies. It was part of the "generic young Seattleite" look, said protester Kevin Scullin. "Living in the Pacific Northwest, we gravitate towards layering clothes for the weather, for warmth and comfort. A cheap black hoodie—we always bought them at Army/Navy surplus—is great for this, with the added utility of having a head covering on hand. Hoodies are also a perfect canvas for adornment, so the anarchist kids could throw up their Crass and other crust band back patches; the other punks could cover theirs in band pins; the hippies could paint stuff on them. Mine was plain black, though."[16]

The protesters taught workshops on the WTO's role in workers' and human rights violations, destruction of the environment, and entrenching global poverty. They climbed walls and construction cranes to hang protest banners. They held potlucks. The following morning, November 30, tens of thousands marched toward the Seattle Convention Center: workers in hard hats and uniforms; children, and adults, costumed as sea turtles; thousands in generic Seattleite hoodies. A few protesters threw garbage cans; other protesters shut them down. Thousands more gathered to sit, stand, link arms, chain themselves, and otherwise block access to the Convention Center, in an act of nonviolent civil disobedience.[17] "It was very festive, though. Music was playing, people were dancing," Scullin said.

Author Wendy C. Ortiz was there too, unhooded but swaddled in a scarf and fuzzy cat-eared hat, in a spirit of "satire and friendly mischief. Knowing I would be out most of the day, I dressed for the cold weather: warm jacket, layers of clothing." And, presciently, goggles. Because the city of Seattle was soon to decide that those hoodies, cat hats, and dancing sea turtles weren't festive or friendly.

At 10:00 a.m. on November 30, the Seattle Police Department, wearing black riot gear, fired tear gas at the peaceful protesters. They drove armored vehicles directly into the crowd; they pepper-sprayed and fired rubber bullets at people.[18] Scullin recalled, "I was seated, with cops about four feet away armed with tear gas canisters and tear gas guns. The canisters hit me right in the foot when they rolled them into the crowd. Keep in mind, this was a huge group of people, stretching city blocks long. You couldn't help but get up and run, when the tear gas hit your face. You can't really see; you just know you're in pain and need to get away. People were tripping and falling over each other, and gathering around folks with water bottles who were cleaning people's eyes."

The Seattle City Council would later state, "Tear gas is a cruel implement to use against persons trying to make deeply-felt statements against what they view as injustice." They concluded that there should be only one legitimate city response to nonviolent protest: nonviolent enforcement. With Northwestern inflection, they added that the police would "have been wiser just to let citizens stand in the rain rather than force dispersal with gas and other means."[19]

That was not what the city did, though. The police clamped down on waves of newly arrived marchers. "People put their hoods up in defense, covered their faces with bandanas. It heightened the sense of solidarity for me," said

Scullin. "The hoodie became a crappy prophylactic against the tear gas and rubber pellets." The Clinton administration insisted that Mayor Paul Schell "clear out" the protesters. The city declared a civil emergency and a downtown no-protest curfew zone; it called in the National Guard. At 5:00, riot police drove everybody out of the zone with rubber bullets and gas, and pursued fleeing protesters into the Capitol Hill neighborhood.

Wendy Ortiz said, "Seeing tanks in the streets of Seattle, police in full riot gear protecting the political players of the WTO as well as property in downtown Seattle, watching tear gas being launched, flash grenades thrown, all underlined for me the abuse of police force in the face of nonviolent protest. Still, I was in a state of disbelief moving through the streets, seeing something I had never experienced firsthand before. The police used and abused the powers they were given."

But ask a pundit, or anybody else who wasn't there, and you'll likely hear a different story, a mangled version of what happened at Starbucks. What really did happen: nearly two hours *after* the SPD had started attacking peaceful protesters, a group of 100–250 black-hooded, bandannaed activists arrived in the shopping area four blocks away. Within thirty minutes, they'd smashed the windows of Starbucks, Bank of America, McDonald's, NIKETOWN, and other businesses. Then, still anonymous, without further incident, they escaped. The police and the press went wild with false reports (later discounted by the City Council) of black-hooded anarchists throwing Molotov cocktails, rocks, and excrement at cops.[20] Municipal and media lies accused the activists of having provoked the police violence that was already well underway. (So persuasive was this narrative that, although Ortiz wasn't involved, her mother, watching the coverage from Los Angeles, was sure she'd recognized her daughter smashing the Starbucks.)

That was how the black bloc entered mainstream US consciousness.

The first black bloc, so named ("Schwarzer Block") by West Berlin police, was deployed by German *Autonomen*, the ideologically diverse environmentalist, feminist, anti-nuclear, and/or anti-racist activists who, in 1980, peacefully occupied a nuclear waste facility construction site, building a little village and sharing food donated by local farmers. One night, 8,000 riot police—the biggest German police mobilization since World War II—invaded the encampment. The protesters tried to sit in but were violently evicted. The following year, when riot police used similar tactics against protesters at the Brokdorf nuclear plant, they encountered a black-masked/hooded resistance that really did throw Molotov cocktails.[21]

Black blocs are not organizations, but strategies, consensus-based actions that coalesce, remix, and dissipate. At large global protests, black blocs have resulted in the use of symbolic force against institutions that create and benefit from injustice (including the police); targeted property destruction; the use of self-defense against state violence; the staging of distractions to deflect police violence away from more vulnerable activists; trash collecting and cleanup; the administering of first aid; charming collaborations with puppet-and-glitter "pink blocs," which are often queer and feminist; and the protection of the police infiltrating their marches. They can be anarchist, ideologically mixed, or unaffiliated; they vary from bloc to bloc and protest to protest. Black blocs sometimes succeed in stymying the workings of capitalism and law enforcement, or in attracting attention to causes (positive or adverse; some media people call a demonstration without "trashing" a "non-event"). What all black blocs signify is the presence of hooded, masked protesters whose autonomous, radical critique is unaccountable to the leaders of larger dissent movements.[22]

Not only state authorities, but also other protesters sometimes oppose their tactics. Black bloc activists' independence, and unaccountability, can undermine solidarity, mask gender and racial insensitivity (there are important critiques of black bloc brocialism), and otherwise disrupt the hard work of principled nonviolence, including both civil disobedience and protest within the framework of permits and policing. That some black bloc protesters engage in property destruction or physical resistance becomes fraught, in light of the unequally shared vulnerability of protesters.

With that said, even the controversial use of such force is markedly disproportionate to the violence of state and corporate powers. It's a felony to smash windows, but not for corporations to contract overseas labor at starvation wages or lobby to gut labor and environmental protections. Rob Walton was not gassed or shot with rubber bullets for the 1,129 people killed at Rana Plaza. (For that matter, the US annually celebrates the 1773 destruction of corporate property in Boston Harbor as a patriotic act. And in the early twentieth century, English suffragists destroyed a great many shop windows, committed arson, and attempted bombings, all of which arguably won them the vote.) Even when some black blocs fight back, their use of force is minimal compared to the authorities' employment of ammunition, tasers, batons, horses, dogs, water cannons, tear gas, and flash bombs against even the most peaceful protesters. In 2000, 150 students sitting in for garment workers' rights at the University of Wisconsin-Madison were pepper-sprayed and assaulted. At the global justice protests of the 2001 G8 Summit in Genoa, a police officer shot black bloc protester Carlo Giuliani in the head at close range. Also at Genoa, 200 masked riot police attacked journalists, doctors, nurses, and protesters sleeping in a school, breaking their bones, beating them unconscious, threatening rape, and denying them access to medical treatment, food, or their consular officials.[23]

At the Seattle WTO protests, the duality of hoods was apparent: riot police concealed their badges under black-hooded ponchos. This use of hoods by authorities would be echoed in the hooding of Greek riot police in 2008, and the governmental deployment of hooded provocateurs, whose acts served to "justify" police crackdowns on protest, in Mexico City in 2014. There's also a long history of the use of hooded collaborators and informers, such as the ghostly, white-hooded *gakunia* in Kenya in the 1950s, and the Filipino Makapili, pro-Japanese militants who wore handwoven palm-leaf bag-hoods during WWII.[24] In Seattle, the black-hooded police pursued thousands of fleeing, nonviolent black-hooded protesters—again, not black bloc members—into Capitol Hill. Ortiz said, "A crowd of people were running away from downtown, and someone was blasting Jimi Hendrix's rendition of 'The Star-Spangled Banner' as we were running, projectiles hitting the ground, flash bangs whipping the crowd into a confused frenzy. It was surreal and terrifying." Seattle police abuse blurred distinctions between protesters, press, legal observers, and bystanders in black hoodies coming home from work or ordering take-out: all found themselves outlaws, vulnerable to pursuit, gassing, or shooting. Tear gas seeped into apartments and restaurants.[25]

Under these circumstances, it was hardly surprising that people who hadn't previously protested began to raise their own black hoods, to defend themselves, escape, show support to the cause—or protest the ongoing police brutality.

It is the duty of the State to protect the constitutional right of people to gather freely which is undermined and hampered by the violence of those who are hooded.

—GREEK MINISTRY OF JUSTICE,
"Measures to Protect Public Peace," issued after the 2008 protests

*You have been warned by the Ku Klux Klan! There will be
consequences for your acts of violence against the peaceful,
law abiding citizens of Missouri.*

—**THE KLAN,**
*claiming the support of the Ferguson
police department, in 2014[26]*

Why write now about the hoodies of the Battle of Seattle?

After Seattle, some critics' takeaway was that the black
bloc had delegitimized the global justice movement. The
government, media, and public were happy to recast the
police brutality as a righteous battle against hoodlums, to
curtail civil liberties with the excuse of protecting citizens,
and to scapegoat the black bloc for inciting violence. Maybe
these criticisms revealed that the black bloc had a necessary
function after all: to expose the pitfalls of "good" and "bad"
dissent rhetoric. At its best, that rhetoric queries how black
blocs' unaccountability can harm and hamper dissent; it
also explores how healthy dissent can allow for multiple
approaches, radicalism, unruliness, disagreement, and
mistakes, too. At its worst, that rhetoric exonerates both
the armed authorities committing violence and the people
who justify that violence. The rhetoric has facilitated the past
decade's deployment of immense ideological and financial
capital, not to mention weaponry, to militarize the police
and to criminalize protest. It enables what David M. Perry
calls the "cult of compliance," by which "police explain away
their actions by citing noncompliance. They do it because

it works. They do it because according to their beliefs, any sign of noncompliance is an invitation to strike."[27] Hooding is noncompliance. Dissent is noncompliance. Anything can be read as noncompliance.

In this context, some reject the black hood. But as Kevin Scullin said about his black hoodie in Seattle, "If I'm in a fight with the police, I'd like to be covered up, for safety, and for anonymity. Before they let the tear gas fly, the cops were blatantly videotaping us, even when we were just sitting." Some choose to reclaim the black hood, along with the protections, fellowships, and subversive and ordinary meanings it can offer. Across many platforms, nations, and climates, protesters stick to their hoods for freedom of movement and speech, for anonymity and self-defense, and simply to assert the right to wear hoods. Black-hooded protesters have demonstrated at the 2004 Republican National Convention in New York; in Spain and in Greece, where they were called the "koukoulofóroi," or the "hooded"; in the Occupy movement; the Brazilian World Cup protests; and the Egyptian revolutionary Black Bloc. And wherever the *V for Vendetta* Guy Fawkes mask meets a hood, from Anonymous protests to the spectacular pairing of Fawkes with hijab, when women protested in Bahrain in 2013 (George Cruikshank was rolling in his grave). And in Iguala, Mexico, where marchers, some in hoodies, some in *pasamontañas*, protested the disappearance of forty-three students kidnapped by what first appeared to be a coalition of city hall, police, and cartel, but was later shown to involve the Mexican federal police and military, who obtained cartel confessions under torture.[28] With such forces arrayed against freedom, concealment is sometimes the dissenter's only defense; sometimes, the only hope of escaping with her life.

If a hood provides inadequate defense against surveillance, civil liberties violations, or a rain of rubber or live bullets, it still invites us to rethink our assumptions about violence and dissent. When peaceful, hooded protesters are assaulted by police hooded in riot gear, heads of state and the public at large ought to hold themselves accountable. They should question the popular ideologies of dissent, criminality, and order that divide "legitimate" protest from "illegitimate," liberal from anarchist, reformist from revolutionary. They should also question how this rhetoric serves racism and other bigotries: for example, the pervasive use of the terms "rioters" and "looters," rather than "radical dissenters," to describe the young people of color, many in hoodies, who protested the 2005 electrocution of three boys during a police pursuit in the Paris *banlieues*—the 2011 police killing of Mark Duggan in London—and the 2015 killing of Freddie Gray in Baltimore, Maryland.[29]

As Norm Stamper, Chief of the Seattle PD in 1999, later wrote:

> Seattle might have served as a cautionary tale, but instead, US police forces have become increasingly militarized, and it's showing in cities everywhere. . . . The paramilitary bureaucracy and the culture it engenders—a black-and-

white world in which police unions serve above all to protect the brotherhood—is worse today than it was in the 1990s. Such agencies inevitably view protesters as the enemy. And young people, poor people and people of color will forever experience the institution as an abusive, militaristic force—not just during demonstrations but every day, in neighborhoods across the country.[30]

The rhetoric of Seattle should be familiar at every protest from Hong Kong to Ferguson: it's the protesters' fault, the hooded ones' fault. It's their fault that the police weren't nice. It's their fault they got beaten, gassed, and shot. Seattle should have exposed the hypocrisy of a culture that holds hooded protesters to standards of superhuman restraint, yet exonerates the hooded police for showing no restraint at all. It's a culture that values compliance with authority over freedom, justice, and people's lives.

4 "IT'S WHAT'S UNDER THE HOOD THAT COUNTS"

The Disinherited Knight had exchanged his armour for the long robe usually worn by those of his condition, which, being furnished with a hood, concealed the features, when such was the pleasure of the wearer, almost as completely as the visor of the helmet itself, but the twilight, which was now fast darkening, would of itself have rendered a disguise unnecessary, unless to persons to whom the face of an individual chanced to be particularly well known.

—SIR WALTER SCOTT, Ivanhoe

Who else wears hoods? Everybody. Surpassing the hood's long association with danger is its longer, infinitely varied precedent of fashion and practicality, hoods for all the purposes of our lives. Samurai wore foldable armored hoods, and women of the Azores wore giant, electric-blue, Marie Antoinette–looking *capote e capelo* hooded cloaks well into the twentieth century. Even Goya, that chronicler of hooded persecution and belief, painted people wearing completely innocuous, weather-appropriate hoods and veils in *The Snowstorm* (1787), and saucy hoods in *Hush* (1797–8). In the 1930s, Martha Graham danced in hooded costumes that resembled fabric tubes; by the late 1960s, everybody was wearing hooded maxi dresses.

And we all wear hoodies. On a 2011 *Newsweek* cover, Sarah "waterboarding is how we baptize terrorists" Palin wore a heather-gray hockey-mom hoodie to announce that she could win the US presidency. In 2006, Sean Combs bedazzled a black-and-white, cotton/polyester-blend hoodie with crystals, for the collection of London's Victoria & Albert Museum. The world's most sublime operatic tenor, Jonas Kaufmann, wore a black hoodie on the cover of his *Winterreise* album, more or less deliberately evoking Romano-British hibernal mosaics. The National September 11 Memorial Museum sells a black "Darkness Hoodie" that proclaims, "In Darkness We Shine Brightest"; after American Giant's Made in the USA hooded sweatshirt (100 percent cotton, streamlined fit, double-lined hood) was proclaimed the "greatest hoodie ever made," the influx of orders resulted in a four-month backlog and the opening of four new stateside factories to sew them.[1]

Even presidents wear hoods. Doro Bush Koch's memoir of her father, George H. W. Bush, captions one photo, "Dad

FIGURE 3 Photograph of George H. W. Bush, reprinted by permission of the George Bush Presidential Library and Museum.

jokes with his staff by wearing a hooded robe during a daily intelligence briefing in 1990."[2] What was so funny—the very fact of his wearing a jellāba? Or was he laughing about the Masonic conspiracy theories that the photo would unleash? All we know is that, should President Bush take a midnight stroll around his neighborhood wearing that hood, the neighborhood watch won't shoot him.

We all wear hoods, donning and doffing them at will, but we can't shed other people's assumptions, hatred, and fear, when they point their fingers, or their guns, saying, "*You are a hood.*"

"Hood, n.3. Etymology: Shortened <NEIGHBOURHOOD n. slang (chiefly U.S., esp. in African-American usage). Freq. with the. A neighbourhood or community, usually one's own; esp. an inner-city area inhabited predominantly by non-whites."

—OXFORD ENGLISH DICTIONARY

On a warm day in January, journalist-educator Andrew J. Padilla, director of the film *El Barrio Tours: Gentrification in East Harlem*,[3] is wearing a hoodie and providing a different definition of the hood. "These are neighborhoods that were killed by the public and private sectors. Redlining segregated them; landlords burned their buildings for insurance money; planned shrinkage closed schools and fire houses. These were calculated attempts to destroy our neighborhoods.

"Gentrification development is a calculated attempt to bring them back—in large part, a P.R. attack. But it's not about bringing up the people, it's about bringing up the property value, and most of the people don't own property or can't afford higher property taxes. This version of 'progress' leads to our exit; in fact, it's conditional on our exit. I used to think gentrification was just white hipsters moving in, paying higher rents, and people of color leaving. As I got older, I realized there were generations of structural racism behind these seemingly natural migrations."

He adds, "Race and economics are inseparable, and you can't expect the media to link the two. Growing up, 90 percent of the media on my neighborhood was from people who didn't come from neighborhoods like these, care for neighborhoods like these, and, unless they needed a janitor, wouldn't hire from neighborhoods like these. There are so many authoritative figures talking who have a borderline disdain for our communities. I got into media-making to tell stories that reflect my reality and that of my community."

A different reality, different community: in 1975, the Council for Public Safety, comprised of New York police and firefighters, published the booklet "Welcome to Fear City: A Survival Guide for Visitors to the City of New York." The front cover featured a black-hooded skull. The booklet advised tourists to "stay away from New York City if you possibly can," but, as "some New Yorkers do manage to survive and even to keep their property intact," tourists should follow their lead by not going out at night, walking, taking the subway, or leaving midtown Manhattan. Their definition of "New Yorkers" included only the Manhattanites shuttling in cabs between doorman buildings, trying their darnedest not to run into the Grim Reaper—who presumably rode the subway in from the Bronx, Brooklyn, or Queens.[4]

There's a gritty 1989 film that captures this epoch of "Fear City." The scene opens in 1977, in downtown Washington Square Park, where a young woman regards a man with wary hostility. He wears a gray hoodie; he carries a baseball bat. But they part without further incident, he to embark on his career as a political analyst, she to write for *The New Yorker*. The man in the hoodie is Billy Crystal; the woman is Meg Ryan; the film is *When Harry Met Sally*.

"Hoodlum, n. Etymology: The name originated in San Francisco about 1870–72, and began to excite attention elsewhere in the U.S. about 1877, by which time its origin was lost, and many fictitious stories, concocted to account for it, were current in the newspapers."

"Hood, n.2. Abbrev. Of HOODLUM n."

Hoods as garments, hoodlums/hoods as people, and neighborhoods don't necessarily have an etymological relationship, but etymologies don't have to be true to have real consequences for people and places. The word "hoodlum" and its 1930s variant "hood" can stick to anybody, so long as somebody else thinks he's a problem. Taking it one step further, the dehumanizing British slur "hoodie," which conflates the garment and the person wearing it (it's fraught even to identify the figure of speech—metonymy?) demonizes a supposed hoodie-wearing type. The "hoodie" is young, male, working class, and/or poor. In the UK, he's often of African or Afro-Caribbean descent, sometimes white or Asian. In the US, he's usually Black, often Latino, and assumed to wear the hoodie for nefarious, antisocial purposes.

In October 2014, Andrew Padilla noticed a sign in a Harlem store window: "DO NOT ENTER WITH HOODIE OR MASK: IF SO YOU ARE NOW TRESPASSING." At the time he'd spotted it, "I'd just come out of a meeting with some people who'd come from Ferguson to Harlem. We were talking about Trayvon Martin, Mike Brown, and how these killings can't keep happening. Then I saw the bodega with the 'no hoodies' sign. It made me think back to the coverage of George Zimmerman's trial."

Padilla had a favorite brown hoodie. "It was comfy, it was casual, it made me feel good, kept me warm. I wasn't wearing it initially as a political statement, it was just an item of clothing. But now, wherever you are, it's a political statement. That's nuts." On that day in October, he pulled his hood up over his head and walked into the store. "I asked the bodegero, 'Hey, did your sign really say no hoodies allowed?' and he got mad uncomfortable: 'Er, um, people wear them to rob us.' I said, 'I could wear a clown mask and rob you. There are so many things I could rob you in.' I tweeted a photo of the sign and put it on my website, and a reporter reached out. There's a guy from Philadelphia selling these signs across the northeast out of his car at ten dollars a pop. There's a market for hate and ignorance. That says a lot: not as much as *American Sniper* grossing more than *Selma* during MLK weekend, but a lot."

The signs were the brainstorm of entrepreneur Joe Stark, who said, "We're trying to put robbers and shoplifters on notice. . . . When you get a guy walking into a store and he has a hood up, a mask up, it can be a scary thing." Stores in New York, Philadelphia, Baltimore, and Washington, DC, posted them; CBS reported, "The store managers we spoke with say it's not hoodies they have a problem with: it's how some people wear them." Such as two Harlem customers, Princess Johnson and her newborn baby, who were both wearing pink hoodies when store management hassled them out: "I can't even get her milk, because they said we're trespassing. So, I feel a little offended," Johnson said.[5]

You can't (legally) ban people from shops or schools because they're Black. You can ban them for wearing hoodies. Over the past decade, several other public and private anti-hoodie initiatives have been proposed, debated, and often implemented, though sometimes defeated, in (not an exhaustive list):

- The Austin, Texas, Public Library, 2010.
- *Stores and business districts*: the Kapiti Coast, New Zealand, 2005. Brisbane, Australia's "Hoodie Free Zone," 2011. Anderson, Indiana, 2014. Philadelphia, Washington, DC, Baltimore, and New York, 2014–15.
  - In 2005, a Kentish mall led the way in mall bans on hoodies, with Tony Blair's endorsement: "It is time to reclaim the streets for the decent majority." The mall also banned leafleting and canvassing.[6]
- *Schools*: Maesteg, Wales, 2005. Meriden, Connecticut, 2007. Andale, Kansas, 2009. Hoboken, New Jersey, 2013. In 2014, Beallsville, Ohio; Jackson County, Florida; and Staten Island, New York.
  - One Portsmouth, Virginia, high school ingeniously banned hoodies on the grounds that they harbored bedbugs. It did not ban such bedbug-harboring objects as shirts,

sweaters, pants, backpacks, desks, light fixtures, or walls.[7]

- – The relationship between hoodies, identity, and free speech was evident in the 2014 one-girl hoodie ban on Saskatchewan eighth-grader Tenelle Starr, of the Star Blanket Cree Nation. Her school forbade her to wear her purportedly "racist," "cheeky," and "rude" fuchsia hoodie printed with the message, "GOT LAND? THANK AN INDIAN."[8]
- • *Cities and states*: Topeka, Kansas, 2012. Castlebar, Ireland, 2013. Oklahoma, 2015.
- • *Nationally*: Greece, 2007.
  - – For a decade in the UK, Anti-Social Behaviour Orders, judicial rulings that punished non-criminal "nuisance" behavior with the threat of fines or jail time, explicitly banned many individuals from wearing hoodies.[9]

When, in 2006, one "over-zealous" UK shopping center guard asked a customer to lower her hood, the incident reached the BBC News. Afterward, the store publicly apologized. Why? For having criminalized a middle-aged, middle-class white woman. "I couldn't believe he was talking to me. I'm supposed to look like a nasty thug?" said hood-wearer Kay Parncutt, adding, "I know now how the youngsters feel to be treated like a criminal for wearing something different. I felt humiliated by the experience, so it must be even worse for teenagers who already encounter problems growing up." Not just teenagers: Rachel Garlinghouse has written about the day a white woman called her Black toddler son a thug.[10]

In 2008, the government of New Zealand attempted to reach out to kids with National Hoodie Day, whose slogan was, "It's what's under the hood that counts." In the Kapiti Coast District, a community board member named Dale Evans protested the holiday by dressing up in a Ku Klux Klan hood and carrying a sign that said, "Its wotz under da hood dat counts." He wasn't the only protester; MP Ron Mark denounced the holiday, saying, "It is so inflammatory and incites the wrath of the average Kiwi out there who is struggling to deal with the tagging on their streets and the gang culture of some young people who use the hoodie, who use black American rap culture as their theme."[11]

Such assumptions about hoodie-wearers are also rife in histories of the hoodie. In the 1970s and 1980s, so the story goes, Black American graffiti artists, hip-hop fans, and gangs adopted hoodies, not because they looked cool (or warm), but to evade the police, hide their identities, and flaunt their underground/underworld connections. There's no room in this narrative for actual hip-hop artists like Gothic Futurist RAMM:ΣLL:ZΣΣ, who wore a fake-fur-and-plastic robot-insect-samurai hood: graffiti writers were fighting a war, he said, to wrest control of the alphabet, a mission they'd inherited from fourteenth-century hooded monks.[12] The hoodie narrative also doesn't account for the huge influence of sports superstars, or designer Norma Kamali—or the revival of the mid-century Ivy League look for 1980s preppies: the hooded sweatshirts, gabardine windbreakers, and yacht anoraks of the white privileged class, who for roughly a century had been slouching toward "sportswear."

Origin stories for the hoodie's popularity lean hard on stereotypes of urban Black cultures, omitting all these other simultaneous, mutual influences, including the strongest influence of all: branding. (Abercrombie, anybody? Tommy Hilfiger? Nike?) The hoodie belonged to jocks, rappers, fashionistas, Ivy Leaguers, punks, and laborers all at once, but the culture that finally made it a staple of mainstream style was the dangerous underworld of the fashion industry, large-scale garment production, marketing, retail, and vast corporate wealth. As Halifu Osumare says, "The hoodie has become one of those cultural markers of the gangster outlaw. It is part of the construction that happens within capitalism. . . . So now when people see a Black man with a hoodie in the street, it becomes an image of a potential thug or gangster. You have these stereotypical images in mind not of what everyone is actually like but what capitalism has promoted as part of this style trend."[13]

Maybe people would see hoodies differently if they adopted the Saskatchewan term "bunny hugs" instead.[14] Or, if the bias against young Black men in hoodies presupposed them all to be Yalies. Everybody wears hoods, but nobody's calling President Bush (Yalie!) a hood. "I love wearing hoodies," says Andrew Padilla in Harlem. "I haven't seen the statistics, and I don't know from comparing the closets of white people on the Upper East Side and people in Harlem, who's more likely to wear a hoodie—but I'd venture to say it's a pretty common item of clothing." He adds, "There are lots of crimes happening on Wall Street, but we don't stop and frisk people who wear Brooks Brothers suits. What suit was Sheldon Silver wearing? What kind was Bernie Madoff wearing?"

To be profiled as a hood, hoodlum, or hoodie, a person doesn't need to be a troublemaker or criminal. He doesn't need to be wearing a hoodie. So long as he has an identity that somebody else criminalizes and dehumanizes, all he has to do is exist.

Never wear a hoodie. Ever.

—J. DREW LANHAM,
"The Rules for the Black Birdwatcher"[15]

The Archbishop of York, Dr. John Sentamu, is the first Black bishop and archbishop of the Church of England. In 2000, while he was Bishop of Stepney, he was subjected to his eighth stop by a police officer, ordered to get out of his car, and questioned. It was raining; Dr. Sentamu was wearing a hooded anorak over his white clerical collar. Experiences like these made him take up the cause of hoodies: "Ninety-nine per cent of those who wear hoodies are law-abiding citizens," he averred, while wearing a hoodie of his own.[16]

Chicago talk show host Charles Butler once wrote, "With hoods pulled up and the pants pulled down, these boys have the look of the drive-by shooter, the armed robber and the perpetrator of other heinous crimes seen nightly on cop shows and newscasts."[17] He was writing about the night he nearly attacked his own nephew, who was wearing a hoodie. Respectability politics like him desperately hope that if Black archbishops would just take off their hoodies and wear suits, racial profiling would disappear. But wearing a US$400 suit didn't prevent Richard McIver from being hauled from his car, pinned, and cuffed by cops policing the 1999 Seattle WTO protests. "All they were interested in was that I was a black man who wasn't doing what they wanted. . . . I've been treated like a nigger before, and that's what this is like."[18] McIver wasn't a protester; he wasn't wearing a hoodie. In fact, he was a member of the Seattle City Council, on his way to a WTO reception at the Westin Hotel.

The respectability of being a councilmember (like mine, Jumaane D. Williams, cuffed and detained by police for walking on a Brooklyn sidewalk), a chaired Harvard professor like Henry Louis Gates, or the second most senior bishop of the Anglican church and an ex-officio member of the House of Lords like Dr. Sentamu, doesn't save people of color from racial suspicion, profiling, stop-and-frisk, and other white supremacist acts. People who have less privilege are even more likely to face, and be blamed for, the unjust treatment they experience. Being a member of a marginalized racial, ethnic, religious, or gender group,[19] working-class or poor, homeless, or an undocumented immigrant; having a developmental disability or illness; or living in a violent neighborhood, can all be attributes of need, vulnerability, and inequality. People with greater privilege often judge these attributes as criminal and deviant, citing them to justify violence against the victims. (A 1992 report on the LAPD found that officials used the term NHI, "no humans involved," to describe cases involving young Black men.)[20] One bitter irony of the objectification of "hoodies" is that, the more disadvantaged and precarious people's lives are, the more likely they are to want to hide from hostile attention and violence. (Butler's nephew had turned up his hood defensively, out of fear.) In turn, the more likely they are to be blamed for wearing the garments they can afford and require for invisibility and self-defense.

In 2006, UK Conservative leader David Cameron gave what would be dubbed the "hug-a-hoodie" speech:

> The fact is, it's frightening for a man in a suit to walk down certain streets at night. But think how much more frightening it must be for a child. . . . Because the fact is that the hoodie is a response to a problem, not a problem in itself. We—the people in suits—often see hoodies as aggressive, the uniform of a rebel army of young gangsters. . . . For me, adult society's response to the hoodie shows how far we are from finding the long-term answers to put things right.[21]

Critics pilloried his speech as soft on crime and a sentimental campaign sound bite, both of which were beside the point. It was a classic "compassionate conservative" maneuver to justify the defunding of social programs, and four years later, Cameron's government would do just that. Cameron's remarks vacillated between the clumsy and the evilly disingenuous, but one part of his speech was haunting. "For young people, hoodies are often more defensive than offensive. They're a way to stay invisible in the street. In a dangerous environment the best thing to do is keep your head down, blend in, don't stand out."

The Venetian letter writer, Laura, understood the need for invisibility. So did the activists of Seattle, Berlin, and Iguala. So do young, poor people, especially those who are people of color. Especially those who are Black. For one moment, Cameron showed empathy for hoodies living in a world that frightens children, and, indeed, many adults of color; he called for government, law enforcement, and the world at large to respond to them with "a lot more love." Who would be alive today, if those powers had actually taken Cameron at his word?

On a drizzly evening, February 26, 2012, one teenager in a hoodie tried to make himself invisible, to keep his head down in a dangerous environment. "That man's following me," he told his friend over the phone. "I'm going to run." He never made it home.[22]

> Black boy has skin like the night sky,
> carries the world and wear it as a hoodie.
> He is decorated with bullet wound stars,
> and people aren't wishing on them.
> —**MARIAM COKER**, from her poem "Comets"[23]

Trayvon Martin's hoodie was the everyday hoodie that anybody might wear. He wore it for his own purposes, whether for staying warm and dry in the rain, for feeling comfortable, for looking casual or cool or ordinary—or, in the last resort, for trying to flee a stalker. That his hoodie came to mean something else was not of his doing, and that's precisely why it matters. The history of the hood is a history of power and powerlessness. It's about acts of hatred, domination, and destruction, but also of control over what exactly people's hoods, and their lives, mean. To define, reduce, criminalize, dehumanize, and objectify; to rob people of the power to determine the meaning and value of their own words, actions, and choices: the meaning of Trayvon Martin's hoodie was stolen from him, just as surely as his life was stolen.

What his hoodie did *not* mean: although Geraldo Rivera, far from the last apologist for Trayvon's murder, said, "His hoodie killed Trayvon Martin as surely as George Zimmerman did," let's get this straight: the hoodie didn't kill him. Roxane Gay compared Rivera's comments to the derailment of asking what women are wearing when they're raped; she added, "Trayvon could have been wearing a My Little Pony t-shirt and George Zimmerman would have perceived the young man as a threat." It was not a murder weapon; it was not an invitation to violence; it was not a justification. It was not even the point. Trayvon's friend Rachel Jeantel said it straight: "It was racial. Let's be honest, racial. If Trayvon was white and he had a hoodie on, would that happen?"[24]

This is not to say, as well-meaning fumblers have said, that Trayvon died because he was Black. Blackness didn't pull that trigger. The "racial" element resided within George Zimmerman, who saw a young Black man in a hoodie and profiled him: in Zimmerman's view, there was something "suspicious," something inherently "wrong with him." Within the context of this "racist narrative of fear and frenzy," George Yancy wrote, "Zimmerman was guilty of an act of aggression against Trayvon Martin, even before the trigger was pulled. Before his physical death, Trayvon Martin was rendered 'socially dead' under the weight of Zimmerman's racist stereotypes."[25]

"What was George Zimmerman wearing when he shot Trayvon Martin?" asked Gay.

The rhetorical uses of Martin's hoodie revealed not his attributes, but those of the people who committed, rationalized, and exonerated the shooting of an unarmed teenager walking home, and the people in the media who repeatedly referred to Martin as the defendant, not the victim. And those who shot at gun targets printed in the boy's image, minus the boy: Skittles, Arizona drink can, and a black hoodie, empty of his face, the crosshairs aimed at his chest. And those who invented "Trayvoning": reenacting Martin's murder, dressing up in hoodies, posing as though shot, and posting the photos online. Martin's hoodie didn't kill him—but these people's hoodies rendered him "socially dead" all over again.[26]

They weren't the only ones live-action roleplaying. In 2014, one year after George Zimmerman's acquittal,

Zimmerman's parents and siblings were living in a state of self-induced siege, in a "safe house." They'd armed themselves against reprisals, such as the time that George's brother Robert was "almost" attacked at Starbucks, and the time a supermarket employee refused to make George a sandwich. They told reporter Amanda Robb that George's biggest fear was that, should he be charged with federal civil rights violations and the "FBI agents come and kick in his door, he's probably gonna shoot a few of them." When Robb tried to visit their house, they decided that *they'd feel safer if she wore a hood*. Robb wrote, "I did tell them that I thought the hood seemed a little Abu Ghraib-y, so we compromised on a blindfold."[27]

The minstrelsy didn't stop there. The people who manipulated and fantasized about Martin's body—spreading lies about his height, weight, and sobriety, editing and misidentifying photos of him—played the victim, and they played the role of enforcers, too. Indulging in the roles of both executioners and martyrs, they insisted on their prerogative to defend themselves—or go on the offense—against villainous thugs in hoodies. They weren't racist—*honi soit qui mal y pense!*—they were reasonable: they simply objected to the idea that Zimmerman's killing of Martin, the police's negligence, the media coverage, or the jury's acquittal needed to be, as they put it, politicized or racialized. But what some people call common sense looks an awful lot like privilege, rationalization, denial, and white supremacy. It was white supremacy that made people demand apologies from President Obama for saying, "If I had a son, he'd look like Trayvon." White supremacy is responsible for the systemic devaluation of Black and Brown people's lives, and for the fact that their harassment, suffering, and murder at the hands of law enforcement represent not states of exception, but rather the state of the nation. As Ta-Nehesi Coates writes, "The injustice was authored by a country which has taken as its policy, for the lionshare of its history, to erect a pariah class. The killing of Trayvon Martin by George Zimmerman is not an error in programming. It is the correct result of forces we set in motion years ago and have done very little to arrest." And as Michael Hanchard says, "For other times, places and peoples, this form of collaboration might have been called fascist, fascism, or fascistic (Germany, Spain, Italy, Uganda) or authoritarian (Brazil, Chile, Argentina), but such words dare not be associated with American exceptionalism—the US experiment with democracy."[28]

Sometimes unjust systems kill, sometimes they exonerate, and sometimes they scold. The apologists, deniers, and perpetrators have lots of advice about what Black and Brown people should and shouldn't do: they should be grateful when the authorities send in more police, in riot gear, to keep the "peace" in communities already devastated by police brutality. They shouldn't consider violence a racial issue and shouldn't demand systemic change. Trayvon Martin shouldn't have been one of the countless people wearing hoodies on that rainy night; he shouldn't have had a sugar craving. Michael Brown shouldn't have walked in the street. Nicholas Heyward (thirteen years old) and Tamir Rice (twelve) shouldn't have been playing; Darrien Hunt shouldn't have cosplayed. Oscar Grant shouldn't have ridden the train; Sandra Bland, Samuel DuBose, Miriam Carey, Shelly Frey, Walter Scott, Jayson Tirado, Timothy Russell, and Malissa Williams shouldn't have driven. Jonathan Ferrell and Renisha McBride shouldn't have needed help after car accidents. Dante Parker and Victor Steen shouldn't have ridden bikes. Akai Gurley and Timothy Stansbury shouldn't have taken the stairs. Kenneth Chamberlain's heart monitor shouldn't have gone off. Anthony Baez shouldn't have thrown a football. Rekia Boyd, James Brissette, Marlon Brown, Patrick Dorismond, Freddie Gray, Kimani Gray (thirteen), Kendrec McDade, Tyisha Miller, Victor White III, and Antonio Zambrano-Montes shouldn't have gone out; Aaron Campbell, Ramarley Graham, Yvette Smith, Tarika Wilson, Aiyana Stanley-Jones (seven), Kathryn Johnston (ninety-two), and Pearlie Golden (ninety-three) shouldn't have been at home; Margaret LaVerne Mitchell shouldn't have been homeless. John Crawford shouldn't have shopped for s'mores ingredients. Michael Stewart shouldn't have been an artist; Ousmane Zongo shouldn't have sold art. Jordan Davis shouldn't have played music. Reynaldo Cuevas shouldn't have fled robbers; Ronald Madison shouldn't have fled gunshots. Sean Bell shouldn't have been getting married. Amadou Diallo shouldn't have tried to show ID. Kayla Moore and Islan Nettles shouldn't have come out as trans women. Tanisha Anderson, Mohamed Bah, Eleanor Bumpurs, Michelle Cusseaux, Ezell Ford, Shereese Francis, Jason Harrison,

Anthony Hill, Dontay Ivy, Natasha McKenna, Iman Morales, Matthew Ojibade, and Kajieme Powell shouldn't have had mental illnesses. Eric Garner shouldn't have stopped breathing.

This is why the hood matters: because it *doesn't* matter in the way Rivera meant. It was Trayvon's hoodie, for him to wear as he liked—to own it, to own its meaning, to own the freedom with which, wearing it, he'd moved through the world. But his killer, and those who collude with and excuse such killers, took it up as both cloak and battle flag. They used and still use it to suppress the truth about bigotry, violence, and injustice. As they've done before, they use it to hoodwink, to invent dubious justifications, to blame violence upon its victims, to deflect attention and outrage, to prevent any change from happening. They use the hood, among all those other excuses, to blame murder on the men, women, and children who die, their bodies, hoodies, habits, and existences. They might as well claim that the victims have up and killed themselves. Move on. Nothing to see here.

The hoodie matters every time people see a Black boy in a hoodie and remember only their own loathing and fear, and not the defenseless child who died.

Which side are you on?

—FLORENCE PATTON REESE'S

union song, which inspired the "Requiem for Mike Brown"

The history of hoods is that of people going about their daily lives, only to face pain and injustice. It's also the history of people determining whose lives do and don't count, who is or isn't human, what is or isn't an object. One man wears a hoodie for his billion-dollar company's IPO. Others wear pro-cop hoodies printed with the message "I CAN BREATHE" at a march for Eric Garner.[29] Detective Richard Zuley led a campaign of brutality in the Chicago Police Department, and got hired to torture hooded prisoners at Guantánamo. Police restrained Natasha McKenna with shackles and a mesh spit hood over her face, before tasering her, until her heart stopped beating. Trayvon's hoodie, arms spread wide like the Man of Sorrow's, was exhibited by the prosecutors at Zimmerman's trial.[30] As Patricia J. Williams writes:

> The line between human and subhuman, or person and thing, is urgently important, particularly in an era when the limits of incarceration, torture, human trafficking, medical experimentation, and the right to due process often turn on newly-minted meanings of words like "enemy combatant," "underclass," "rational actor," "terrorist," or "illegal alien." . . . The immediacy of human need may be overshadowed by inanimate objects as the exclusive repositories of our protective anxiety and fear.[31]

Those who back the torturers and executioners wield immense power to decide whose lives matter and what they mean, but they are never the only ones to make those claims. Mamie Till-Mobley subverted the practice of lynching photography by publishing photos of her murdered son, Emmett: "The whole nation had to bear witness to this." Sybrina Fulton said of her son, "The verdict is not going to define who Trayvon Martin was. We will define his legacy." Wyclef Jean, Young Jeezy, Willie D, Plies, Alicia Keys, The Game, J. Cole, Lauryn Hill, the Rising Sun All Stars, and the singers of the "Requiem for Mike Brown" memorialized lost lives and demanded action. People wear hoodies in dissent: the Miami Heat, the Million Hoodies, the legislators who donned protest hoodies at the US House of Representatives and New York State Senate, and those who take to the streets now. Peopling their hoodies, they reject the empty-faced targets, the figments of racist imagination, to declare that Black Lives Matter.[32]

The history of the hood remembers the murdered children, lynching victims, shot protesters, prisoners of war and the prison-industrial complex, and genocide victims. This history isn't about ranking or falsely equating their experiences, but about rejecting what Christina Sharpe calls a "zero-sum approach to how we conceptualize questions of social justice that face our democracy—that your gain must mean my concomitant loss." Because two gay men, the Black poet Langston Hughes and the white artist Prentiss Taylor, collaborated on the anti-lynching "Christ in Alabama." Because a Filipino-American major general accused the Bush administration of war crimes against Arab and Muslim prisoners. Because a young woman activist, smiling under her *keffiyeh*, can bear a sign saying "Ferguson with love from Palestine" while protesters in both places endure the same brand of tear gas.[33] These stories corroborate each other, mounting evidence in the cases against hatred and injustice.

In Tony Kushner's play *Angels in America*, Prior Walter, abandoned, terrified, and dying of AIDS, decides to hood himself like the Grim Reaper: "Prior is dressed oddly; a great long black coat and a huge, fringed, matching scarf, draped to a hoodlike effect. His appearance is disconcerting, menacing and vaguely redolent of the Biblical." Black-hooded and dying, Prior is not, however, an agent of death. He wrestles an angel to win admission to Heaven. Once there, he demands more life, for himself and for all the other sufferers abandoned by God.

> PRIOR: I want more life. I can't help myself. I do.
> I've lived through such terrible times, and there are people who live through much much worse, but . . . . You see them living anyway. . . . We live past hope. If I can find hope anywhere, that's it, that's the best I can do. It's so much not enough, so inadequate but . . . . Bless me anyway. I want more life.[34]

Sometimes a hood is just a hood, and sometimes it heralds the end of days, but always, it frames someone's face. So long as we all wear hoods, so long as we experience privilege or precarity in them, we're forced into the struggle between the humanizers and the objectifiers, between vulnerable lives and the reduction of people to objects. Knowing this, we might decide to insist on life—to demand more life—in these terrible times: that's the object lesson of the hood.

ACKNOWLEDGMENTS

Bottomless gratitude to Christopher Schaberg, Ian Bogost, and Haaris Naqvi for welcoming this book in their series: I'm honored. Thanks to Alice Marwick for the wonderful cover; thanks to wordsmith Susan Clements, Mary Al-Sayed and James Tupper at Bloomsbury, Anita Singh at Deanta Global, and my agent Laura Blake Peterson and Marnie Zoldessy at Curtis Brown Ltd. For heroism in reading and improving the manuscript, Moustafa Bayoumi, Ellen V. Holloman, Patricia A. Matthew, Asa Simon Mittman, Susan Nakley, Julie Orlemanski, David M. Perry, Jesús Rodríguez-Velasco, Stuart Schrader, and Christy Thornton. For sharing their stories, Wendy C. Ortiz, Andrew J. Padilla, and Kevin Scullin. For hood lore and help, Nicole Antebi, Yasmin Belkhyr, Paul Benzon, Dianne Berg, Alex Branch, Eric Breault, Samir Chopra, Colin Dickey, Karen Gregory, Mobina Hashmi, Anne Harris, Stuart L. Hartstone at Florida Capital Resource Center, Katherine Ibbett, Jennifer Kabat, Danielle L. Kellogg, Ariana Kelly, Kathleen E. Kennedy, Paula Lee, Marieke Lewis, Gabriel Liston, Bess Lovejoy, Michele Mittman, Nita Noveno,

Oona Patrick, Lydia Pyne, Judd Tully, Aurélie Vialette, and Michael R. Zimmerman. For the work that inspired and shaped this book, the activists, artists, writers, and scholars. For research and editorial support, listening, talking, and reading with me about all the hoods in this book, and for everything else, Karl Steel, whose contributions to this project are legion.

Selections (pp. 33, 133) from *Angels in America, Part Two: Perestroika*, by Tony Kushner. Copyright © 1992, 1994, 1996 by Tony Kushner, published by Theatre Communications Group. Used by permission of Theatre Communications Group.

Selection from *The Executioner's Song*, by Norman Mailer, reprinted by permission of the Norman Mailer Licensing Company.

Selection from *The Last Face You'll Ever See*, by Ivan Solotaroff. Copyright © 2001 by Ivan Solotaroff, reprinted by permission of HarperCollins Publishers and The Friedrich Agency.

Selection from "The Wasteland," by T. S. Eliot, reprinted by permission of Faber and Faber Ltd.

Selections republished with permission of West/Wadsworth, from *Death Work: A Study of the Modern Execution Process*, Robert Johnson, 2nd edition, 2005; permission conveyed through Copyright Clearance Center, Inc.

LIST OF
ILLUSTRATIONS

NOTES

Epigraph

1 Bobby L. Rush, "A Hood on the Head Does Not Mean a Hoodlum in the Head," *Rush.house.gov*, March 28, 2012, http://rush.house.gov/press-release/hood-head-does-not-mean-hoodlum-head.

Chapter 1

1 Anna Wintour, "Signs of the Times," *Vogue,* July 2004: 30.

2 R. S. O. Tomlin, "Voices From the Sacred Spring," in *Bath History*, ed. Trevor Fawcett, vol. IV (Bath, UK: Millstream Books, 1992), 16.

3 Roger Ling, "The Seasons in Romano-British Mosaic Pavements," *Britannia* 14 (January 1, 1983): 16; Sara Lipton, *Dark Mirror: The Medieval Origins of Anti-Jewish Iconography* (New York: Metropolitan Books, 2014), 17; John Mandeville, *The Egerton Version of Mandeville's Travels*, trans. M. C. Seymour (New York: Oxford University Press, 2010), 132.

4 Maureen C. Miller, *Clothing the Clergy: Virtue and Power in Medieval Europe, c. 800–1200* (Ithaca: Cornell University Press, 2014), 17, 44.

5 *Saint Francis and Crowned Death* (c. 1300–1320), attributed to the Maestro delle Vele d'Assisi or Pietro Lorenzetti; Bernt Notke, *Reval Dance of Death* (after 1463); Lavaudieu *La Mort noire* (after 1355); Heinrich Knoblochtzer, *Der doten dantz* (1488); Hans Sebald Beham, *Death and the Maiden* (1546); *Arundel Psalter* (c. 1310–1320). For a hot Friday night, stay home with: Philippe Ariès, *Images of Man and Death*; Paul Binski, *Medieval Death: Ritual and Representation*; Enrico De Pascale, *Death and Resurrection in Art*; Clifton C. Olds, Ralph G. Williams, and William R. Levin, *Images of Love and Death in Late Medieval and Renaissance Art*.

6 Maxence Grugier, "Gremlins, Alien, Goldorak : Les Étranges Chimères de La Chapelle Bethléem," *Gentside*, January 17, 2013, http://fluctuat.premiere.fr/Diaporamas/Gremlins-Alien-Goldorak-les-etranges-chimeres-de-la-Chapelle-Bethleem-3637884.

7 Elina Gertsman, *The Dance of Death in the Middle Ages: Image, Text, Performance*, (Turnhout, Belgium: Brepols Publishers, 2010), 169; "Was the Cauld Lad murdered after all?" *Sunderland Echo*, November 28, 2007, http://www.sunderlandecho.com/what-s-on/was-the-cauld-lad-murdered-after-all-1-1141690.

8 Maare E. Tamm, "Personification of Life and Death Among Swedish Health Care Professionals," *Death Studies* 20, no. 1 (February 1996): 10, 14.

9 Paul Sendziuk, "Denying the Grim Reaper: Australian Responses to AIDS," *Eureka Street*, 2002, http://www.eurekastreet.com.au/articles/0310sendziuk.html.

10 Ivan Solotaroff, *The Last Face You'll Ever See: The Private Life of the American Death Penalty* (New York: HarperCollins, 2001), 27, 47. A representative of the Florida DOC confirmed over the phone that, as of September 8, 2015, the executioner still uses the hood at every execution.

11 Robert Johnson, *Death Work: A Study of the Modern Execution Process*, 2nd ed. (Belmont, CA: West/Wadsworth, 1998), 137.

12 Ron Word, "Fla. Protects Doctors' IDs," *USAToday.com*, August 28, 2007, http://usatoday30.usatoday.com/news/nation/2007-08-28-3113489692_x.htm.

13 Jonathan Bridges, "Hooding the Jury," *University of San Francisco Law Review* 35 (Summer 2001): 655; Markus Feldenkirchen, "Botched Execution: The Search for a Clean Way of Killing," *Spiegel Online*, September 18, 2014, http://www.spiegel.de/international/world/execution-of-clayton-lockett-and-the-flaws-of-lethal-injection-a-992359-2.html; David Ammons, "Washington Hangman's ID Can Be Kept Secret, Court Rules," *Associated Press*, May 3, 1990, http://www.apnewsarchive.com/1990/Washington-Hangman-s-ID-Can-be-Kept-Secret-Court-Rules/id-c2916284f2898cc7ba0c69333c9467d2.

14 Ellyde Roko, "Executioner Identities: Toward Recognizing a Right to Know Who Is Hiding Beneath the Hood," *Fordham Law Review* 75, no. 5 (2007): 2800, 2806–07, 2811; Chelsea J. Carter and Jason Morris, "Documents: Not Enough Drugs Left to Finish Botched Oklahoma Execution," *CNN*, September 8, 2014, http://www.cnn.com/2014/05/01/us/oklahoma-botched-execution/index.html.

15 Roderick C. Patrick, "Hiding Death," *New England Journal on Criminal & Civil Confinement* 117 (1992): 118; Henry J. Reske, "Who Pulls the Switch? Suit Claims a Right to Know Identity of Florida Executioners," *ABA Journal* 77, no. 11 (November 1, 1991): 38; Jonathan Bridges, "Hooding the Jury," 651; John D. Bessler, *Death in the Dark: Midnight Executions in America*

(Boston: Northeastern University Press, 1997), 150; Johnson, *Death Work*, 125.

16 Benjamin Rush, "Benjamin Rush to Jeremy Belknap, October 7, 1788," in *Belknap Papers*, ed. Ebenezer Hazard, vol. IV (Boston: Massachusetts Historical Society, 1891), 419.

17 Jason Zasky, "The Faithful Executioner," *Failure Magazine*, accessed October 13, 2014, http://failuremag.com/feature/article/the-faithful-executioner/.

18 "22 Marzo 1796: il primo giorno di lavoro di Mastro Titta, il boia di Roma," *Telesanterno*, March 22, 2013, http://www.telesanterno.com/22-marzo-1796-il-primo-giorno-di-lavoro-di-mastro-titta-il-boia-di-roma-0322.html.

19 Petrus Cornelis Spierenburg, *The Spectacle of Suffering: Executions and the Evolution of Repression: From a Preindustrial Metropolis to the European Experience* (Cambridge, UK: Cambridge University Press, 1984), 32, 41.

20 Ruth Mellinkoff, *Outcasts: Signs of Otherness in Northern European Art of the Late Middle Ages*, vol. 1 (Berkeley: University of California Press, 1993), 59–89.

21 Michel Foucault, *Discipline and Punish: The Birth of the Prison*, trans. Alan Sheridan, 2nd Vintage Books ed. (New York: Vintage Books, 1995), 81.

22 Annulla Linders, "The Execution Spectacle and State Legitimacy: The Changing Nature of the American Execution Audience, 1833–1937," *Law & Society Review* 36, no. 3 (2002): 635, 643; Louis P. Masur, *Rites of Execution: Capital Punishment and the Transformation of American Culture, 1776–1865* (New York: Oxford University Press, 1989), 4, 51–4, 97, 112.

23 Albert R. Carman, "Wall Paintings in Europe," *The Canadian Magazine* (1906): 308.

24 Robert Mills, *Suspended Animation: Pain, Pleasure and Punishment in Medieval Culture* (London: Reaktion, 2005), 13–14.

25 Cesare Vecellio and Ambroise Firmin Didot, *Costumes anciens et modernes*, IV, vol. 1 (Typographie de Firmin Didot Frères Fils & Cie, 1859), fig. 143.

26 Nicholas Terpstra, "Piety and Punishment: The Lay Conforteria and Civic Justice in Sixteenth-Century Bologna," *The Sixteenth Century Journal* 22, no. 4 (Winter 1991): 679–94.

27 Norman Mailer, *The Executioner's Song* (Boston: Little, Brown & Company, 1979), 871.

28 "History of Eastern State Penitentiary, Philadelphia," accessed January 6, 2015, http://www.easternstate.org/learn/research-library/history; "England With All Her Faults," *The Westminster Review* CXXIX (June 1888): 621.

29 Johnson, *Death Work*, 133–4.

30 Siméon Prosper Hardy, *Mes loisirs*, ed. Maurice Tourneux and Maurice Vitrac (Paris: A. Picard, 1912), 327.

31 Johnson, *Death Work*, 176, 121.

32 John Bell, "The Sioux War Panorama and American Mythic History," *Theatre Journal* 48, no. 3 (October 1996): 280, 283.

33 Linders, "Execution Spectacle," 634; Michael D. Crews, "Michael D. Crews to The Honorable Rick Scott, September 9, 2013," September 9, 2013, http://www.dc.state.fl.us/oth/deathrow/lethal-injection-procedures-as-of_9-9-2013.pdf; "They Shoot Horses, Don't They?" *Time*, October 8, 1973.

34 Dwight Conquergood, "Lethal Theatre: Performance, Punishment, and the Death Penalty," *Theatre Journal* 54, no. 3 (October 2002): 352.

35 Jerry Givens, "I Was Virginia's Executioner from 1982 to 1999. Any Questions for Me?" *TheGuardian.com*, November 21, 2013, http://www.theguardian.com/commentisfree/2013/nov/21/death-penalty-former-executioner-jerry-givens.

36 Helen Prejean, *Dead Man Walking: An Eyewitness Account of the Death Penalty in the United States* (New York: Vintage Books, 1993), 101.

37 Linders, "Execution Spectacle," 620; Foucault, *Discipline and Punish*, 62, 64; Spierenburg, *Spectacle*, 102.

38 Samuel Danforth, "The Cry of Sodom Enquired Into; Upon Occasion of the Arraignment and Condemnation of Benjamin Goad, for His Prodigious Villany. (1674) An Online Electronic Text Edition," ed. Paul Royster, *Faculty Publications, UNL Libraries* (1674), 13–14, 16–17, http://digitalcommons.unl.edu/libraryscience/34.

39 Frances E. Dolan, "'Gentlemen, I Have One Thing More to Say': Women on Scaffolds in England, 1563–1680," *Modern Philology* 92, no. 2 (November 1994): 173–4.

40 Michael A. Trotti, "The Scaffold's Revival: Race and Public Execution in the South," *Journal of Social History* 45, no. 1 (Fall 2011): 205–21.

41 Conquergood, "Lethal Theatre," 362–4.

42 Lesley Clark, "Florida Execution of 350-Pound Inmate Turns Bloody," *Miami Herald*, July 8, 1999, http://www.clarkprosecutor.org/html/death/US/davis558.htm; "ACLU Calls for Moratorium After Gruesome Electric Chair Execution," *American Civil Liberties Union*, July 8, 1999, https://www.aclu.org/capital-punishment/aclu-calls-moratorium-after-gruesome-electric-chair-execution.

43 Sean Wilentz, "Crime, Poverty and the Streets of New York City: The Diary of William H. Bell, 1850–51," *History Workshop*, no. 7 (Spring 1979): 148.

44 William Edmundson, *A Journal of the Life, Travels, Sufferings, and Labour of Love in the Work of the Ministry, of That Worthy Elder and Faithful Servant of Jesus Christ, William Edmundson, Who Departed This Life, the Thirty-First of the Sixth Month, 1712*, 3rd ed. (Dublin, UK: Christopher Bentham, 1820), 148.

45 "Iraq: Amnesty International Deplores Death Sentences in Saddam Hussein Trial," *Amnesty International*, November 5, 2006, http://www.amnesty.org/en/library/asset/MDE14/037/2006/en/0292f7f1-f9d1-11dd-b1b0-c961f7df9c35/mde140372006en.pdf; "Witness: Saddam Hussein Argued with Guards Moments before Death," *CNN*, December 30, 2006, http://www.cnn.com/2006/WORLD/meast/12/30/hussein/index.html?eref=rss_latest.

46 Ahmer Nadeem Anwer, "The Noose, the Hegemon and the Apostate Body: Spectacular Transformations of the Scaffold," *Social Scientist* 35, no. 3/4 (April 2007): 100.

47 Mills, *Suspended Animation*, 27; Christopher Hitchens, "Lynching the Dictator," *Slate*, January 2, 2007, http://www.slate.com/articles/news_and_politics/fighting_words/2007/01/lynching_the_dictator.html.

48 Prejean, *Dead Man Walking*, 21; Masur, *Rites of Execution*, 14–15, 122–3.

Chapter 2

1 Lianna Hart, "3 Charged in Texas After Black Man's Grisly Death," *LATimes.com*, June 10, 1998, http://articles.latimes.com/1998/jun/10/news/mn-58507.

2 Ariel Kaminer, "Coney Island Sideshow Has Guantánamo Theme," *NYTimes.com*, August 5, 2008, http://www.nytimes.com/2008/08/06/arts/design/06wate.html?pagewanted=all&_r=0.

3   Site's down; see the mirror site www.oocities.org/kkk_kbay/
    page1.html.tmp.

4   Dore Ashton, *A Critical Study of Philip Guston* (Berkeley, CA:
    University of California Press, 1990), 31.

5   Ellen G. Landau, "Double Consciousness in Mexico: How
    Philip Guston and Reuben Kadish Painted a Morelian Mural,"
    American Art 21, no. 1 (Spring 2007): 75.

6   Nancy S. Cannon, "Reform/Conflict: The Anti-Rent
    Movement: Brief Introduction," *Voice of the People: Life in the
    Antebellum Rural Delaware County New York Area*, http://
    www.oneonta.edu/library/dailylife/protest/; Elaine Frantz
    Parsons, "Midnight Rangers: Costume and Performance in the
    Reconstruction-Era Ku Klux Klan," *The Journal of American
    History* 92, no. 3 (December 2005): 818–21.

7   *Testimony Taken By the Joint Select Committee To Inquire Into
    the Condition of Affairs in the Late Insurrectionary States:
    Georgia*, vol. VI: I (Washington: Government Printing Office,
    1872), 237; *South Carolina*, vol. IV: II, 695–6, 681–3.

8   Parsons, "Rangers," 823–36.

9   Ralph Blumenthal, "Fresh Outrage in Waco at Grisly
    Lynching of 1916," *NYTimes.com*, May 1, 2005, http://www.
    nytimes.com/2005/05/01/national/01lynch.html; "August
    7, 1930: A Night of Terror," *The Indianapolis Star*, March
    17, 2011, http://archive.indystar.com/article/20110320/
    ENTERTAINMENT/103200309/Aug-7-1930-night-
    terror; Philip Dray, *At the Hands of Persons Unknown: The
    Lynching of Black America* (New York: Modern Library,
    2002), xi, 13, 78.

10 Dora Apel, "Torture Culture: Lynching Photographs and the
    Images of Abu Ghraib," *Art Journal* 64, no. 2 (Summer 2005):
    90–1.

11 Kathy Sawyer, "A Lynching, a List and Reopened Wounds; Jewish Businessman's Murder Still Haunts Georgia Town," *The Washington Post*, June 20, 2000, http://www.lexisnexis.com. ez-proxy.brooklyn.cuny.edu:2048/hottopics/lnacademic/.

12 Ray Stannard Baker, "The Negro in Politics," *The American Magazine*, vol. LXVI (New York: The Phillips Publishing Company, 1908), 177.

13 Dray, *Persons Unknown*, x, 125.

14 Julie Buckner Armstrong, *Mary Turner and the Memory of Lynching* (Athens, GA: University of Georgia Press, 2011), 26, 38, 53–7, 149; Hugh M. Dorsey, "Hugh M. Dorsey to John R. Shillady, November 30, 1918," November 30, 1918, http://www.maryturner.org/images/Dorsey.pdf.

15 "48,000 People in Great Griffith Film," *The Daily Constitution*, November 1, 1924, http://access.newspaperarchive.com. ez-proxy.brooklyn.cuny.edu:2048/us/missouri/chillicothe/chillicothe-constitution/1924/11-01/page-2?.

16 Michael Rogin, "'The Sword Became a Flashing Vision': D. W. Griffith's The *Birth of a Nation*," *Representations* 0, no. 9 (Winter 1985): 171.

17 Drake Stutesman, "Clare West," *Women Film Pioneers Project*, September 27, 2013, https://wfpp.cdrs.columbia.edu/pioneer/ccp-clare-west.

18 Charles O. Jackson, "William J. Simmons: A Career In Ku Kluxism," *The Georgia Historical Quarterly* 50, no. 4 (December 1, 1966): 352; Charles C. Alexander, "Kleagles and Cash: The Ku Klux Klan as a Business Organization, 1915–1930," *The Business History Review* 39, no. 3 (October 1, 1965): 349, 353–4; Tom Rice, "'The True Story of the Ku Klux Klan': Defining the Klan through Film," *Journal of American Studies* 42, no. 3 (December 1, 2008): 473.

19 Ku Klux Klan, *Catalogue of Official Robes and Banners* (Atlanta: Knights of the Ku Klux Klan Inc., 1925), http://archive.org/details/catalogueofoffic00kukl; Jon Blackwell, "1924: Hatred Wore a Hood in Jersey," *The Capital Century*, accessed December 15, 2014, http://capitalcentury.com/1924.html.

20 Hrag Vartanian, "Relics of Slavery and Hate, on Display in New York," *Hyperallergic*, July 17, 2014, http://hyperallergic.com/138399/the-relics-of-slavery-and-hate-on-display-in-new-york/.

21 Armstrong, *Mary Turner*, 70, 102.

22 Harold Brackman, "The Attack on 'Jewish Hollywood': A Chapter in the History of Modern American Anti-Semitism," *Modern Judaism* 20, no. 1 (February 1, 2000): 10.

23 Landau, "Double Consciousness," 82–3.

24 John F. Chuchiak IV, ed. and trans., *The Inquisition in New Spain, 1536–1820: A Documentary History* (Baltimore: The John Hopkins University Press, 2012), 144–8.

25 Richard L. Kagan and Abigail Dyer, eds., *Inquisitorial Inquiries: Brief Lives of Secret Jews and Other Heretics* (Baltimore: The Johns Hopkins University Press, 2004), 11–18, 183; Irene Silverblatt, "Heresies and Colonial Geopolitics," *Romanic Review* 103, no. 1–2 (2012): 75–7.

26 Anorak, "The Story of the Klu Klux Klan in Pictures: Racism, Civil Rights and Murder," *Flashbak*, December 10, 2012, http://flashbak.com/the-story-of-the-klu-klux-klan-in-pictures-racism-civil-rights-and-murder-13893/.

27 Richard E. Greenleaf, *The Mexican Inquisition of the Sixteenth Century* (Albuquerque: University of New Mexico Press, 1969), 51–3.

28 "Trial of the Jews of Trent, Manuscript, 1478," *Center for Jewish History*, accessed January 14, 2015, http://www.cjh.org/collectionhighlights/2; Landau, "Double Consciousness," 76, 83, 90–1.

29 Gudmund Lindbaek, "Holy Week: Jesus, Mary and Antonio Banderas," *King Goya*, April 15, 2014, http://www.kinggoya.com/holy-week-in-malaga-jesus-mary-and-antonio-banderas/.

30 Samuel K. Cohn, "The Black Death and the Burning of Jews," *Past & Present* 196 (August 2007): 8, 12.

31 Silvana Seidel Menchi, "Characteristics of Italian Anticlericalism," in *Anticlericalism: In Late Medieval and Early Modern Europe*, eds. Peter A. Dykema and Heiko A. Oberman (Leiden: E. J. Brill, 1993), 278.

32 Lynn Hunt, Margaret C. Jacob, and Wijnand Mihnhardt, *The Book That Changed Europe* (Cambridge, MA: The Belknap Press of Harvard University Press, 2010), 196.

33 Silverblatt, "Heresies," 65–7; Horswell, "Negotiating Apostasy," 81; José Rabasa and Jesús Rodríguez-Velasco, "Introduction," *Romanic Review* 103, no. 1–2 (2012): 6.

34 http://www.zazzle.com/spanish+inquisition+ornaments. The Dupin ornament is no longer available, but you can still buy Goya's.

35 Henry Charles Lea, *A History of the Inquisition of Spain*, vol. 3, Book 6 (New York: Macmillan, 1906).

36 Hugh Barclay and I. S. H. Laidlaw, eds., *The Journal of Jurisprudence*, vol. 28 (Edinburgh: T. T. Clark, 1884), 106.

37 Pamela Branch, *The Wooden Overcoat* (Boulder, CO: The Rue Morgue Press, 2006), 10.

38 "U.N. Rights Mission Flies to Meet U.S. Prisoner in Peruvian Prison," *NYTimes.com*, January 29, 1998, http://www.nytimes.

com/1998/01/29/world/un-rights-mission-flies-to-meet-us-prisoner-in-peruvian-prison.html.

39 Michael P. Scharf, "Can This Man Get a Fair Trial?" *WashingtonPost.com*, December 19, 2004, http://www.washingtonpost.com/wp-dyn/articles/A9481-2004Dec17.html.

40 Hector Mondragon, "I Too Was Tortured," *SOA Watch*, accessed January 12, 2015, http://www.soaw.org/component/content/article/1/2123.

41 Darius Rejali, *Torture and Democracy* (Princeton, NJ: Princeton University Press, 2007), 279, 290, 320.

42 The International Military Tribunal for Germany, *Trial of the Major War Criminals Before the International Military Tribunal*, vol. 6 (The Avalon Project, 1996), http://avalon.law.yale.edu/imt/01-25-46.asp.

43 Andrée Dore-Audibert, *Des Françaises d'Algérie dans la guerre de libération: des oubliées de l'histoire* (Paris: Éditions Karthala, 1995), 69.

44 Martha K. Huggins, Mika Haritos-Fatouros, and Philip G. Zimbardo, *Violence Workers: Police Torturers and Murderers Reconstruct Brazilian Atrocities* (Berkeley: University of California Press, 2002), 166, 185, 259.

45 Marguerite Feitlowitz, *A Lexicon of Terror: Argentina and the Legacies of Torture* (New York: Oxford University Press, 2011), 62.

46 Mark Bowden, "The Dark Art of Interrogation," *TheAtlantic.com*, October 1, 2003, http://www.theatlantic.com/magazine/archive/2003/10/the-dark-art-of-interrogation/302791/; Rejali, *Torture*, 337, 340, 355; Human Rights Watch/Middle East, *Torture and Ill-Treatment: Israel's Interrogation of Palestinians from the Occupied Territories* (New York: Human Rights Watch, 1994), 129.

47 Bowden, "Interrogation."

48 George W. Bush, "Humane Treatment of Al Qaeda and Taliban Detainees," February 7, 2002, http://www2.gwu. edu/~nsarchiv/NSAEBB/NSAEBB127/02.02.07.pdf; Judith Butler, "Torture and the Ethics of Photography," *Environment and Planning D: Society & Space* 25, no. 6 (December 2007): 951–66.

49 Clare Monagle and Louise D'Arcens, "'Medieval' Makes a Comeback in Modern Politics: What's Going On?" *TheConversation.com*, September 22, 2014, http:// theconversation.com/medieval-makes-a-comeback-in-modern-politics-whats-going-on-31780; Tom Lasseter, "Day 4: Easing of Laws That Led to Detainee Abuse Hatched in Secret," *McClatchyDC*, June 18, 2008, http://www.mcclatchydc. com/2008/06/18/38886_day-4-easing-of-laws-that-led. html?rh=1.

50 Committee on Armed Services, US Senate, "Inquiry Into the Treatment of Detainees in U.S. Custody: Report of the Committee on Armed Services," November 20, 2008, 136, http://www.armed-services.senate.gov/imo/media/doc/ Detainee-Report-Final_April-22-2009.pdf.

51 Mohamedou Ould Slahi, "Guantánamo Diary: 'I Saw the Cockpit. I Saw the Guards. I Saw the Ghosts of My Fellow Detainees,'" *TheGuardian.com*, January 16, 2015, http://www. theguardian.com/world/2015/jan/16/-sp-guantanamo-diary-flight-saw-cockpit-saw-guards-saw-ghosts-of-fellow-detainees.

52 Steven G. Bradbury, "Memorandum for John Rizzo, Acting General Counsel of the Central Intelligence Agency," August 1, 2002, 2, 4, 28, http://s3.amazonaws.com/ nytdocs/docs/151/151.pdf; US Senate Select Committee on Intelligence, "Committee Study of the Central Intelligence Agency's Detention and Interrogation Program Together with

Foreword by Chairman Feinstein and Additional and Minority Views (S. Rpt. 113-288)," December 9, 2014, 41–2, http://www.intelligence.senate.gov/study2014/executive-summary.pdf.

53 Lt. Col. Diane E. Beaver, "Memorandum for Commander, Joint Task Force 170," October 11, 2002, 6, http://www2.gwu.edu/~nsarchiv/NSAEBB/NSAEBB127/02.12.02.pdf.

54 "Translation of Statement Provided by Abdou Hussain Saad Faleh, Detainee #18470, 1610/16 JAN 04," trans. Abdelilah Alazadi, January 16, 2004, http://www.washingtonpost.com/wp-srv/world/iraq/abughraib/swornstatements042104.html?g.

55 Philip Gourevitch and Errol Morris, *Standard Operating Procedure* (New York: The Penguin Press, 2008), 155.

56 W. J. T. Mitchell, *Cloning Terror: The War of Images, 9/11 to the Present* (Chicago: University of Chicago Press, 2011), 157.

57 Susan Sontag, "Regarding The Torture Of Others," *The New York Times Magazine*, May 23, 2004, http://www.nytimes.com/2004/05/23/magazine/regarding-the-torture-of-others.html; W. J. T. Mitchell, "The Unspeakable and the Unimaginable: Word and Image in a Time of Terror," *ELH* 72, no. 2 (Summer 2005): 304; Patricia J. Williams, "In Kind," *TheNation.com*, May 13, 2004, http://www.thenation.com/article/kind.

58 Gourevitch and Morris, *Standard Operating Procedure*, 71.

59 Nicole Archer, "Security Blankets: Uniforms, Hoods, and the Textures of Terror," *Women & Performance: A Journal of Feminist Theory* 24, no. 2–3 (December 6, 2014): 3.

60 Gourevitch and Morris, *Standard Operating Procedure*, 154, 227; Seymour M. Hersh, "The General's Report,"

NewYorker.com, June 25, 2007, http://www.newyorker.com/
magazine/2007/06/25/the-generals-report.

61 Major General Antonio M. Taguba, "AR 15-6 Investigation of
the 800th Military Police Brigade," February 26, 2004, 16–18,
http://www.dod.mil/pubs/foi/operation_and_plans/Detainee/
taguba/TAGUBA_REPORT_CERTIFICATIONS.pdf; Luke
Harding, "After Abu Ghraib," *TheGuardian.com*, September 20,
2004, http://www.theguardian.com/world/2004/sep/20/usa.
iraq.

62 Errol Morris, "The Most Curious Thing," *NYTimes.com*, May
19, 2008, http://opinionator.blogs.nytimes.com/2008/05/19/
the-most-curious-thing/.

63 Adam Hochschild, "What's in a Word? Torture," *NYTimes.
com,* May 23, 2004, http://www.nytimes.com/2004/05/23/
opinion/what-s-in-a-word-torture.html.

64 Sontag, "Torture"; Taguba Report, 25.

65 Butler, "Torture," 963; Lisa Hajjar, "An Army of Lawyers,"
TheNation.com, December 7, 2005, http://www.thenation.
com/article/army-lawyers#.

66 The Editors, "Conspiracy to Torture," *TheNation.com*,
December 8, 2005, http://www.thenation.com/article/
conspiracy-torture.

67 Steven Watt, "Outsourced Terror: The Horrific Stories of
CIA-Sponsored Torture That Aren't in the Senate Report,"
Slate, December 19, 2014, http://www.slate.com/articles/
news_and_politics/politics/2014/12/senate_torture_
report_s_unnamed_victims_the_cia_had_hundreds_or_
thousands.html; Jonathan Horowitz and Stacy Cammarano,
"20 Extraordinary Facts about CIA Extraordinary
Rendition and Secret Detention," *Open Society Foundations*,

February 5, 2013, http://www.opensocietyfoundations.org/
voices/20-extraordinary-facts-about-cia-extraordinary-
rendition-and-secret-detention.

68 Major General Antonio Taguba (Ret.) and Physicians for
Human Rights, "Report Preface," in *Broken Laws, Broken
Lives: Medical Evidence of Torture by US Personnel and
Its Impact* (Physicians for Human Rights, 2008), http://
physiciansforhumanrights.org/library/reports/broken-laws-
torture-report-2008.html; Naomi Klein, "'Never Before!' Our
Amnesiac Torture Debate," *TheNation.com*, December 8,
2005, http://www.thenation.com/article/never-our-amnesiac-
torture-debate#.

69 Errol Morris, "Will the *Real* Hooded Man Please Stand Up,"
NYTimes.com, August 15, 2007, http://opinionator.blogs.
nytimes.com/2007/08/15/will-the-real-hooded-man-please-
stand-up/?_r=0.

70 "Get the Data: Drone Wars," *The Bureau of Investigative
Journalism*, accessed January 28, 2015, http://www.thebureau
investigates.com/category/projects/drones/drones-graphs/.

71 Dora Apel, *War Culture and the Contest of Images*
(New Brunswick, NJ: Rutgers University Press, 2012), 80.

72 Hamza Hendawi, "Images of Iraqi Prisoners Used in Art,"
AP, May 8, 2004, http://www.electricrequiem.com/forum/
showthread.php?3289-Images-of-Iraqi-Prisoners-Used-
In-Art; Negar Mottahedeh, "Off the Grid: Reading Iranian
Memoirs in Our Time of Total War," *Middle East Research and
Information Project*, September 2004, http://www.merip.org/
mero/interventions/grid; Apel, *War Culture*, 70–1.

73 Virginie Locussol, "US Prison Abuse Painted on Wall," *Middle
East Online*, January 6, 2004, http://www.middle-east-online.
com/english/?id=10129.

Chapter 3

1   David W. Blight, *Race and Reunion: The Civil War in American Memory* (Cambridge: Harvard University Press, 2001), 37, 291.

2   Vicente L. Rafael, "Parricides, Bastards, and Counterrevolution: Reflections on the Philippine Centennial," in *Vestiges of War: The Philippine-American War and the Aftermath of an Imperial Dream 1899–1999*, ed. Angel Velasco Shaw and Luis H. Francia (New York: New York University Press, 2002), 365; Teodoro A. Agoncillo, *The Revolt of the Masses* (Quezon City: University of the Philippines, 1956), 50–1; Rene G. Ontal, "Fagen and Other Ghosts: African-Americans and the Philippine-American War," in *Vestiges of War*, 122–5.

3   Michael J. Horswell, "Negotiating Apostasy in Vilcabamba: Titu Cusi Yupanqui Writes from the *Chaupi*," *Romanic Review* 103, no. 1–2 (2012): 93.

4   A. T. Hatto, trans., *The Nibelungenlied* (New York: Penguin Books, 1969), 54; Sarah Beach, "Robin Hood and Green Arrow: Outlaw Bowmen in the Modern Urban Landscape," in *Robin Hood in Popular Culture: Violence, Transgression, and Justice*, ed. Thomas G. Hahn (Cambridge, UK: Boydell & Brewer, 2000), 23; Jack Zipes, *The Trials and Tribulations of Little Red Riding Hood: Versions of the Tale in Sociocultural Context* (South Hadley, MA: Bergin & Garvey Publishers, Inc., 1983), 290.

5   James H. Johnson, *Venice Incognito: Masks in the Serene Republic* (Berkeley and Los Angeles, CA: University of California Press, 2011), 149–51.

6 Susie Khamis, "Braving the Burqini™: Re-Branding the Australian Beach," *Cultural Geographies* 17, no. 3 (July 1, 2010): 384; "From Bikini to 'Burqini,'" *The Sydney Morning Herald*, January 16, 2007, http://www.smh.com.au/news/fashion/burqini-comes-to-aussie-beaches/2007/01/16/1168709713446.html.

7 Geoff Harkness and Samira Islam, "Muslim Female Athletes and the Hijab," *Contexts* 10, no. 4 (Fall 2011): 65; Uriya Shavit and Ofir Winter, "Sports in Contemporary Islamic Law," *Islamic Law & Society* 18, no. 2 (May 2011): 270–1.

8 "IDF: le 'burkini' interdit à la piscine," *Le Figaro*, August 12, 2009, http://www.lefigaro.fr/flash-actu/2009/08/12/01011-20090812FILWWW00302-le-burkini-interdit-a-la-piscine-de-meaux.php; Angelique Chrisafis, "Why Speedos Are Still Huge in France," *TheGuardian.com*, August 11, 2009, http://www.theguardian.com/lifeandstyle/2009/aug/12/speedos-fashion; "Une femme interdite de piscine pour cause de 'burqini,'" *LeMonde.fr*, August 12, 2009, http://www.lemonde.fr/societe/article/2009/08/12/une-femme-interdite-de-piscine-pour-cause-de-burqini_1228075_3224.html; Monique Keller, "Quand la burqa fusionne avec le bikini," *Tribune de Genève*, March 18, 2008, http://archives.tdg.ch/actu/suisse/2008/03/18/burqa-fusionne-bikini.

9 UK company Modestly Active made Lawson's suit; Madeleine Bunting, "Nigella Lawson and the Great Burkini Cover-Up," *TheGuardian.com*, April 22, 2011, http://www.theguardian.com/lifeandstyle/2011/apr/23/nigella-lawson-burkini-bikini-swimming.

10 Dietmar Hipp and Maximilian Popp, "Islam in Germany: Burqini Ruling Was the Right Call," *Spiegel Online*, December 9, 2013, http://www.spiegel.de/international/germany/

commentary-german-court-made-right-call-on-gym-class-burqini-ruling-a-921862.html.

11 Veronica Dewar, "Keynote Address: Our Clothing, Our Culture, Our Identity," in *Arctic Clothing*, eds. J. C. H. King, Birgit Pauksztat, and Robert Storrie (Montreal and Kingston: McGill-Queen's University Press, 2005), 25–6; Michael R. Zimmerman, Anne M. Jensen, and Glenn W. Sheehan, "Agnaiyaaq: The Autopsy of a Frozen Thule Mummy," *Arctic Anthropology* 37, no. 2 (2000): 54; Rhoda Akpaliapik Karetak, "Amautiit," in *Arctic Clothing*, 80–1.

12 Pauktuutit Inuit Women's Association and Phillip Bird, *Inuit Women's Traditional Knowledge Workshop on the Amauti and Intellectual Property Rights: Final Report* (Ottawa: Pauktuutit Inuit Women's Association, 2002), 18, 37–51, http://www.wipo.int/export/sites/www/tk/en/igc/ngo/amauti_report.pdf.

13 T. S. Eliot, "The Waste Land," *The Complete Poems and Plays of T. S. Eliot* (London: Faber and Faber Limited, 1969), 73.

14 Kirst, Sean, "The History of the Hoodie: Upstate Invention, Practical Intention," *The Post-Standard*, December 27, 2009, http://www.syracuse.com/kirst/index.ssf/2012/04/post_263.html.

15 "Sixty Big Name Brands Continuing to Use Sweatshop Labour," *Thejournal.ie*, May 3, 2011, http://www.thejournal.ie/60-big-name-brands-continuing-to-use-sweatshop-labour-130318-May2011/; Jeff Ballinger, "Finding an Anti-Sweatshop Strategy That Works," *Dissent* 56, no. 3 (Summer 2009): 5.

16 Thanks to Kevin Scullin and Wendy C. Ortiz (wendyortiz.com) for their personal communications on November 19 and 25, 2014, respectively.

17 WTO Accountability Review Committee of the Seattle City Council, "History/Timeline," October 19, 2000, http://www.seattle.gov/archive/wtocommittee/history.htm; "Day Two," *The WTO History Project*, http://depts.washington.edu/wtohist/day2.htm.

18 Alex Tizon, "Monday, Nov. 29," *SeattleTimes.com*, December 5, 1999, http://community.seattletimes.nwsource.com/archive/?date=19991205&slug=2999667.

19 WTO Accountability Review Committee, "Accountability Review Committee Final Report," September 14, 2000, 12, http://www.seattle.gov/archive/wtocommittee/arcfinal_report.htm.

20 Nichole M. Christian, "Police Brace For Protests In Windsor And Detroit," *NYtimes.com*, June 4, 2000, http://www.nytimes.com/2000/06/04/us/police-brace-for-protests-in-windsor-and-detroit.html.

21 Michael McCanne, "Scenes Resembling Civil War," *TheNewInquiry.com*, January 3, 2013, http://thenewinquiry.com/essays/scenes-resembling-civil-war/.

22 Francis Dupuis-Déri, "The Black Blocs Ten Years after Seattle: Anarchism, Direct Action, and Deliberative Practices," *Journal for the Study of Radicalism* 4, no. 2 (Fall 2010): 46–64, 67–77.

23 Allie Robbins, "The Future of the Student Anti-Sweatshop Movement: Providing Access to U.S. Courts For Garment Workers Worldwide," *Labor & Employment Law Forum* 3, no. 1 (January 1, 2013): 124; A. K. Thompson, "You Can't Do Gender in a Riot: Violence and Post-Representational Politics," *Berkeley Journal of Sociology* 52 (2008): 25; Melody Niwot, "Narrating Genoa: Documentaries of the Italian G8 Protests of 2001 and the Persistence and Politics of Memory," *History & Memory* 23, no. 2 (Fall/Winter 2011): 69–70.

24 Marinos Pourgouris, "The Phenomenology of Hoods: Some Reflections on the 2008 Violence in Greece," *Journal of Modern Greek Studies* 28, no. 2 (October 2010): 229, 238; John M. Ackerman, "Mexican Hope," *LatinoRebels.com,* November 11, 2014, http://www.latinorebels.com/2014/11/11/mexican-hope/; Koigi Wa Wamwere, *I Refuse to Die: My Journey For Freedom* (New York: Seven Stories Press, 2002), 88; Clarissa V. Militante, "The hooded witness in Makapili tradition," *GMANewsOnline*, March 14, 2006, http://www.gmanetwork.com/news/story/1981/news/specialreports/the-hooded-witness-in-makapili-tradition.

25 Jeffery Beckstrom, "Interviews with Eyewitnesses," *WTO Accountability Review Committee*, October 19, 2000, http://www.seattle.gov/archive/wtocommittee/interviews.htm; Justin Carder, "WTO 10 Years Later: The Battle for Capitol Hill," *CapitolHillSeattle.com*, November 27, 2009, http://www.capitolhillseattle.com/2009/11/wto-10-years-later-the-battle-for-capitol-hill/.

26 Arturo Garcia, "Ku Klux Klan Leader Defends Threat of 'Lethal Force' against Ferguson 'Terrorists,'" *RawStory.com*, November 12, 2014, http://www.rawstory.com/rs/2014/11/ku-klux-klan-leader-defends-threat-of-lethal-force-against-ferguson-terrorists/.

27 David M. Perry, "Ferguson and the Cult of Compliance," *Al Jazeera America*, August 15, 2014, http://america.aljazeera.com/opinions/2014/8/ferguson-police-shootracismcompliance.html.

28 Christy Thornton and Steve Fisher, "The Federal Police Not Only Knew, They Were There (Audio)," *NACLA*, January 9, 2015, https://nacla.org/news/2015/01/08/federal-police-not-only-knew-they-were-there-audio.

29 David Wright, "Away, Running: A Look at a Different Paris,"
    Callaloo 32, no. 1 (Winter 2009): 7; Claudia Rankine, *Citizen:
    An American Lyric* (Minneapolis: Graywolf Press, 2014),
    114–18.

30 Norm Stamper, "Paramilitary Policing From Seattle to Occupy
    Wall Street," *TheNation.com*, November 9, 2011, http://www.
    thenation.com/article/164501/paramilitary-policing-Seattle-
    occupy-wall-street.

Chapter 4

1   Leah Mirakhor, "The Hoodie and the Hijab: Arabness,
    Blackness, and the Figure of Terror," *Los Angeles Review
    of Books*, June 6, 2015, https://lareviewofbooks.org/essay/
    the-hoodie-and-the-hijab-arabness-blackness-and-the-
    figure-of-terror-james-baldwin; Farhad Manjoo, "The
    Only Problem With the Greatest Hoodie Ever Made," *Slate,*
    March 21, 2013, http://www.slate.com/articles/technology/
    technology/2013/03/american_giant_hoodie_the_only_
    problem_with_the_world_s_greatest_sweatshirt.html.

2   Doro Bush Koch, *My Father, My President: A Personal Account
    of the Life of George H.W. Bush* (New York: Warner Books,
    2006), 426.

3   Thanks to Andrew J. Padilla, andrewjpadilla.com. Interview
    January 23, 2015.

4   Jen Carlson, "The 1970s Pamphlet Aimed At Keeping
    Tourists Out Of NYC," *Gothamist*, September 16, 2013, http://
    gothamist.com/2013/09/16/the_1970s_pamphlet_aimed_at_
    keeping.php.

5   Gustavo Solis, "No Hoodies Allowed in Harlem Businesses, Signs Warn," *DNAinfo.com*, October 27, 2014, http://www. dnainfo.com/new-york/20141027/central-harlem/harlem-businesses-post-sign-telling-people-wearing-hoodies-not-enter/; "Some Harlem Businesses Display 'No Hoodies Allowed' Signs," *CBS New York*, October 27, 2014, http:// newyork.cbslocal.com/2014/10/27/some-harlem-businesses-display-no-hoodies-allowed-signs/.

6   "'Respect' Key to Blair Third Term," *BBC*, May 17, 2005, http:// news.bbc.co.uk/2/hi/uk_news/politics/4554179.stm.

7   "Stephanie Harris Reports on Churchland High Bed Bugs Hoodie Rule," 2013, https://www.youtube.com/watch?v=rRXu DAZqKbo&feature=youtube_gdata_player.

8   ICTMN Staff, "First Nation Student Wins Right to Wear 'Got Land?' Hoodie After School Ban," *IndianCountryTodayMediaNetwork.com*, January 15, 2014, http://indiancountrytodaymedianetwork.com/2014/01/15/ first-nation-student-wins-right-wear-got-land-hoodie-after-school-ban-153120.

9   "ASBOwatch: Monitoring the Use of Anti-Social Behaviour Orders," *Statewatch.org*, accessed November 21, 2014, http:// www.statewatch.org/asbo/ASBOwatch.html.

10 "Shop Regrets 'Hoodie' Humiliation," *BBC*, February 21, 2006, http://news.bbc.co.uk/2/hi/uk_news/england/ wiltshire/4735154.stm; Matt Jackson, "Hoodie-Winked!" *Swindon Advertiser*, February 18, 2006, http://www. swindonadvertiser.co.uk/archive/2006/02/18/691498.Hoodie_ winked/; Rachel Garlinghouse, "To The Lady Who Called My Toddler a Thug," *HuffingtonPost.com*, March 20, 2015, http:// www.huffingtonpost.com/rachel-garlinghouse/to-the-lady-who-called-my-toddler-a-thug_b_6903332.html.

11 "Councillor Slammed for 'Outrageous' Ku Klux Klan
    Costume," *Sydney Morning Herald*, May 30, 2008, http://
    www.smh.com.au/news/world/outrage-at-kiwi-councillors-
    outfit/2008/05/30/1211654268340.html.

12 Paul Benzon, "Afrofuturist Anachrony: Ramellzee and the
    Politics of Media Archaeology for SCMS 2015," May 19, 2015,
    http://paulbenzon.com/afrofuturist-anachrony-rammellzee-
    and-the-politics-of-media-archaeology-for-scms-2015/.

13 "Prep Yourself: A Vintage Ivy-League Style Manual,"
    GQ, August 31, 2010, http://www.gq.com/style/wear-it-
    now/201008/take-ivy-best-prep-style-book-photos; Eric
    Wilson, "Who Put the Black in Black Style?" *NYtimes.com*,
    August 31, 2006, http://www.nytimes.com/2006/08/31/
    fashion/31black.html; Emanuelle Grinberg, "Hoodie's
    Evolution from Fashion Mainstay to Symbol of Injustice,"
    CNN, March 27, 2012, http://www.cnn.com/2012/03/27/
    living/history-hoodie-trayvon-martin/index.html.

14 "Bunny Hugs Fit Province Perfectly," *The Star
    Phoenix*, April 16, 2007, http://www.canada.com/
    saskatoonstarphoenix/news/story.html?id=70fc9c9d-86e4-
    48f4-9d81-6d4079334a66.

15 J. Drew Lanham, "The Rules for the Black Birdwatcher,"
    BirdNote.org, February 2015, http://birdnote.org/
    video/2015/02/rules-black-birdwatcher-j-drew-lanham.

16 Vikram Dodd, "Black Bishop 'Demeaned' by Police Search,"
    TheGuardian.com, January 24, 2000, http://www.theguardian.
    com/uk/2000/jan/24/race.world; "Archbishop Woos Hoodie
    Generation," *BBC*, May 2, 2006, http://news.bbc.co.uk/2/hi/
    uk_news/england/bradford/4962624.stm.

17 Charles Butler, "Hoodie Rights and Responsibilities," *The
    National Leadership Network of Black Conservatives: Project

21, September 6, 2012, http://www.nationalcenter.org/
P21NVButlerHoodies90612.html.

18 J. Martin McOmber, "Councilman Says He Got Degrading
Handling By Police—He Showed His Council Business
Card, But All Officers Saw Was His Race, McIver Says,"
The Seattle Times, December 3, 1999, http://community.
seattletimes.nwsource.com/archive/?date=19991203&sl
ug=2999046.

19 Moustafa Bayoumi, "The Race Is On: Muslims and Arabs in
the American Imagination," *Middle East Report Online*, March
2010, http://www.merip.org/mero/interventions/race.

20 Neil Roberts, "Trayvon Martin: Introduction," *Theory & Event*
15, no. 3 (2012), http://muse.jhu.edu/journals/theory_and_
event/v015/15.3.roberts.html.

21 "Cameron 'Hoodie' Speech in Full," *BBC*, July 10, 2006, http://
news.bbc.co.uk/2/hi/5166498.stm.

22 *Rachel "Dee Dee" Jeantel (W8) Testimony Pt. 1/6*, 2013, http://
trayvon.axiomamnesia.com/people/witnesses/witness-8-files-
trayvon-martin-george-zimmerman-case/.

23 Mariam Coker, "Comets," *Winter Tangerine Review,* February
5, 2015, http://www.wintertangerine.com/comets.

24 Roxane Gay, "A Place Where We Are Everything," *TheRumpus.
net*, March 23, 2012, http://therumpus.net/2012/03/a-place-
where-we-are-everything/; Matt Smith, "Martin Friend 'Upset,
Angry' by Verdict," *CNN*, July 17, 2013, http://www.cnn.
com/2013/07/15/justice/zimmerman-trial-jeantel/.

25 George Yancy, "Walking While Black in the 'White Gaze,'"
NYtimes.com, September 1, 2013, http://opinionator.blogs.
nytimes.com/2013/09/01/walking-while-black-in-the-
white-gaze/.

26 Patricia J. Williams, "The Luminance of Guilt: On Lives through the Lens of Apocalypse," *Transition* 113, no. 1 (2014): 162–9; Christina Sharpe, "Blackness, Sexuality, and Entertainment," *American Literary History* 24, no. 4 (2012): 839.

27 Amanda Robb, "Zimmerman Family Values," *GQ*, October 2014, http://www.gq.com/news-politics/big-issues/201410/george-zimmerman-family-values.

28 Ta-Nehisi Coates, "Trayvon Martin and the Irony of American Justice," *TheAtlantic.com*, July 15, 2013, http://www.theatlantic.com/national/archive/2013/07/trayvon-martin-and-the-irony-of-american-justice/277782/; Michael Hanchard, "You Shall Have The Body: On Trayvon Martin's Slaughter," *Theory & Event* 15, no. 3 (2012), http://muse.jhu.edu/journals/theory_and_event/v015/15.3.hanchard.html.

29 Spencer Ackerman, "Guantánamo torturer led brutal Chicago regime of shackling and confession," *TheGuardian.com*, February 18, 2015, http://www.theguardian.com/us-news/2015/feb/18/guantanamo-torture-chicago-police-brutality; Blue Telusma, "NYPD supporters wear 'I Can Breathe' hoodies to taunt protesters," *TheGrio.com*, December 20, 2014, http://thegrio.com/2014/12/20/nypd-supporters-i-can-breathe-taunt-protesters/.

30 Manuel Roig-Franzia, "What will become of Trayvon's hoodie, the latest piece of iconic trial evidence?" *WashingtonPost.com*, July 30, 2013, http://www.washingtonpost.com/lifestyle/style/what-will-become-of-trayvons-hoodie-the-latest-piece-of-iconic-trial-evidence/2013/07/30/0882de30-f951-11e2-afc1-c850c6ee5af8_story.html.

31 Williams, "Luminance," 169.

32 Steve Edwin, "Remembering the Ancestor's Image: Emmett Till and Predicaments of Witnessing," *Callaloo* 37, no. 3 (2014): 714; Erin Donaghue, "Sybrina Fulton: 'Use My Broken Heart' to Prevent More Deaths like Son Trayvon Martin," *CBS News*, July 26, 2013, http://www.cbsnews.com/news/sybrina-fulton-use-my-broken-heart-to-prevent-more-deaths-like-son-trayvon-martin/; Casey Seiler, "'Hooded' Legislators Make a Point," *Times Union*, March 27, 2012, http://www.timesunion.com/local/article/Hooded-legislators-make-a-point-3435567.php.

33 Ange-Marie Hancock, "Trayvon Martin, Intersectionality, and the Politics of Disgust," *Theory & Event* 15, no. 3 (2012), http://muse.jhu.edu/journals/theory_and_event/v015/15.3.hancock.html; Hamde Abu Rahma, "To Ferguson, with Love from Palestine," August 22, 2014, http://hamdeaburahma.com/2014/08/22/to-ferguson-with-love-from-palestine/.

34 Tony Kushner, *Angels in America, Part Two: Perestroika*, rev. ed. (New York: Theatre Communications Group, Inc., 1996), 33, 133.

INDEX

Page references for illustrations appear in *italics*.